RECOVERY ROOM:

SURVIVING FAMILY ESTRANGEMENT

Anne Stewart Helton, RN, BSN, MS

Photos by Anne Helton

ISBN: 978-1-6999055-8-6
Copyright Registration: TXu 2-150-488

ENDORSEMENTS

Estrangement is a situation often fueled by enablers. *Recovery Room* provides some answers for this unspoken parental grief and it will help readers move forward.
Barbara Bissett

Recovery Room is so well written and describes the feelings I have had in the past…and still have. I haven't seen or spoken to my daughter in over two years. I have no idea where she is…dead or alive. She's just disappeared. Other than all the memories…was our time with her meant to be only a season? My husband and I are letting go. She's left us no choice. **J.B.**

Well worth the read. Everything resonated with me. Thank you so much, Anne Helton, for giving me the words to articulate my journey.
T.

I pray for my estranged child. It's all I can do now. We were close for many years, but now he blames me for all his mistakes and has cut me off. It is like living death. Thank you for describing the estrangement grief model. **B.**

Walking through the land of estrangement can easily qualify as one of the most difficult journeys any parent embarks upon. *Recovery Room* serves as a base map that equips moms and dads to accept and embrace the avalanche of emotions and fashion realistic solutions.

Melanie Stiles, Life Coach

To Estranged Parents:
You want answers and directions on how you can rebuild your family. The truth lies inside the human heart and in God's hands. There are no magic answers, however, this book may help you to understand the issues of estrangement a little more, find some paths to restoration, build spiritual strength and, hopefully, have more peace within yourself.
It is this I pray.

Estrange (a transitive verb): To arouse especially mutual enmity or indifference in someone where there had formerly been love, affection, or friendliness...ALIENATE.

Estrangement (noun): The fact of no longer being on friendly terms or part of a social group.

"He hath put my brethren far from me, and mine acquaintance are verily estranged from me."
Job 19:13

DEDICATION

This book is dedicated to all heartbroken parents who have been estranged in one way or another by their adult children. And, also to estranged adult children... May they read it, soften their hearts, rebuild and reunite. Heartfelt hope to those friends who have suffered from family estrangement, shared their pain and support, especially Barbara, who is a wise survivor. And many thanks to my strong daughter, Missy, and my husband, John R. Helton, Sr. who has mended his own heart from the destruction of estrangement and helped to sew mine back together.

Anne Stewart Helton: The Happy Jesus Nurse

In memory of my IrishGrandmother: Catherine M. GallagherStewart, b.1883, Ireland – She always wrote heartfelt poems and stories (typically Irish, with a misspelled mix of English and Gaelic). This was my favorite (speaking prophetically) about a sad, empty old home. It was a time when she and my grandfather, Walter E. Stewart, had raised their seven children on their Stewart Ranch, which sat on the border of California and Mexico. When the poem was written, the ranch home had become run down and empty. This was an old, faded original piece and the drawing was by her daughter, my aunt "Babe"-Angela Stewart.

Poem Transcription

Our old home looked sad in the late autumn sun. The fall wind is blowing so cold

The milk-house and windmill are torn and gone, the barn and bunkhouse are old.

There are no bridles or saddles in the corral; No bronco or pintos in the stalls

Lassoes and spurs are on the scrap pile, the chuck wagon is not there at all.

When we lived there the fields were all green, the cattle and horses well fed. It was always a home for a stranger to call for a meal and sometimes, for a bed.

It's different now, the children all gone, no cattle or horses in the stall. No smoke from the chimney, no smell of fresh bread, no children to come when I call.

We feel like the old buildings, we are now getting shaky, as we watch the sun setting, and we know it is late. So, we listen for the phone and watch for the mailman, and, sometimes we meet him outside the gate.

By Catherine M. Stewart, circa 1950

Contents

RECOVERY ROOM:

SURVIVING FAMILY ESTRANGEMENT

Anne Stewart Helton, RN, BSN, MS

Photos by Anne Helton

ISBN: 978-0-9961309-4-3
Copyright Registration: TXu 2-150-488

ENDORSEMENTS

Estrangement is a situation often fueled by enablers. *Recovery Room* provides some answers for this unspoken parental grief and it will help readers move forward.
Barbara Bissett

Recovery Room is so well written and describes the feelings I have had in the past...and still have. I haven't seen or spoken to my daughter in over two years. I have no idea where she is...dead or alive. She's just disappeared. Other than all the memories...was our time with her meant to be only a season? My husband and I are letting go. She's left us no choice. ***J.B.***

Well worth the read. Everything resonated with me. Thank you so much, Anne Helton, for giving me the words to articulate my journey.
T.

I pray for my estranged child. It's all I can do now. We were close for many years, but now he blames me for all his mistakes and has cut me off. It is like living death. Thank you for describing the estrangement grief model. ***B.***

Walking through the land of estrangement can easily qualify as one of the most difficult journeys any parent embarks upon. *Recovery Room* serves as a base map that equips moms and dads to accept and embrace the avalanche of emotions and fashion realistic solutions.

Melanie Stiles, Life Coach

To Estranged Parents:
You want answers and directions on how you can rebuild your family. The truth lies inside the human heart and in God's hands. There are no magic answers, however, this book may help you to understand the issues of estrangement a little more, find some paths to restoration, build spiritual strength and, hopefully, have more peace within yourself.
It is this I pray.

Estrange (a transitive verb): To arouse especially mutual enmity or indifference in someone where there had formerly been love, affection, or friendliness...ALIENATE.

Estrangement (noun): The fact of no longer being on friendly terms or part of a social group.

"He hath put my brethren far from me, and mine acquaintance are verily estranged from me."
Job 19:13

DEDICATION

This book is dedicated to all heartbroken parents who have been estranged in one way or another by their adult children. And, also to estranged adult children… May they read it, soften their hearts, rebuild and reunite. Heartfelt hope to those friends who have suffered from family estrangement, shared their pain and support, especially Barbara, who is a wise survivor. And many thanks to my strong daughter, Missy, and my husband, John R. Helton, Sr. who has mended his own heart from the destruction of estrangement and helped to sew mine back together.

Anne Stewart Helton: The Happy Jesus Nurse

In memory of my IrishGrandmother: Catherine M. GallagherStewart, b.1883, Ireland – She always wrote heartfelt poems and stories (typically Irish, with a misspelled mix of English and Gaelic). This was my favorite (speaking prophetically) about a sad, empty old home. It was a time when she and my grandfather, Walter E. Stewart, had raised their seven children on their Stewart Ranch, which sat on the border of California and Mexico. When the poem was written, the ranch home had become run down and empty. This was an old, faded original piece and the drawing was by her daughter, my aunt "Babe"-Angela Stewart.

Poem Transcription

Our old home looked sad in the late autumn sun. The fall wind is blowing so cold

The milk-house and windmill are torn and gone, the barn and bunkhouse are old.

There are no bridles or saddles in the corral; No bronco or pintos in the stalls

Lassoes and spurs are on the scrap pile, the chuck wagon is not there at all.

When we lived there the fields were all green, the cattle and horses well fed. It was always a home for a stranger to call for a meal and sometimes, for a bed.

It's different now, the children all gone, no cattle or horses in the stall. No smoke from the chimney, no smell of fresh bread, no children to come when I call.

We feel like the old buildings, we are now getting shaky, as we watch the sun setting, and we know it is late. So, we listen for the phone and watch for the mailman, and, sometimes we meet him outside the gate.

By Catherine M. Stewart, circa 1950

Contents

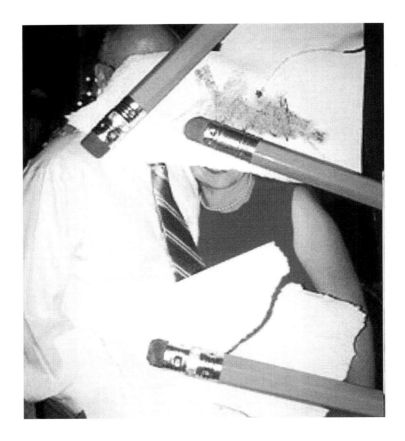

CHAPTER ONE

ERASED MEMORIES:
The Hidden Problem of Estrangement

What does one do when someone you love erases you? What does one do when the history of your life is distorted or recreated? And if it is someone you thought loved you? Someone you birthed? Someone you nurtured and raised? Up to now, I have avoided being specific about this issue and how it has impacted me, but perhaps my thoughts and experiences will help others with this growing problem. I'm not talking about erased memories from Alzheimer Disease, dementia, head injury or stroke; I'm talking about a deliberate, take- you-out-of-their-heads-and-hearts type of action, a rearranging of history. It sounds crazy, right? But it happens around us every day. I have come to realize there is **nothing** that can be done about this sad situation unless both sides want to fix it. So, rule one is this: Parents, stop beating yourselves up!

This curse is the pain of family estrangement and all of the characters in this type of family drama know their lines well. They play their chosen roles. They enter and exit stage left with a smile or a tear and they can even construct plot points one and two and completely turn the drama around...especially if they have a *Greek chorus,* an audience, to take sides, root for them, and cheer and cry at the twists and turns.

With any estrangement there is **never** and **always** a reason for the estrangement, depending on who is doing the talking, but especially when the players grip tightly their grudge ropes and hang on. This is especially true if any of the parties stay stuck in the *"and then he said this and then she did that"* mode of life but also if secondary gains are received for the act of estranging. As for me, my adult child has decided that he had a bad childhood. His father and I know it's not true, but it took us a while to get to a place of peace about it. We know that we raised him, beginning as teenage parents, with all the love we had in our hearts, with all the time, nurturing, work, money and devotion possible, giving him guidance and educational experiences well into adulthood. We had fun with him, cheering him on as he played sports, excelled in school, developed his many gifts, especially his sense of humor. Even when he became an adult and went through some bumps in life, we were always there for him in every way possible. Mistakes made? Yes, but wouldn't everyone love to turn back time as wisdom is gained?

Our son, a writer, has intermittently decided that his reality was different from ours. He has talked and written about it. Like many estranged parents, we have finally realized there is nothing we can say, do or ask, to change that. *So much time lost.* Through the years, we have *"taken the high road"* when his words have hurt us, like when we stayed up late at night just to hear his voice on the radio speaking about his new writings or accomplishments only to hear him eventually blame any troubles or poor decisions on us, his parents. We have anonymously gone to book signings, standing in the back, to see and hear him speak and support him, but then left when he took a negative turn. Most recently we watched him on C-Span talk about his latest book and he was very interesting. We loved hearing his passion and heart.

But then we heard him describe that he had a bad childhood and that reading books helped him escape from it; sadly, he laughed, as the narrator prompted and validated the response from him. He had a choice to recant, but he smirked as he verbally *threw us under the bus* again and effectively ran over us and the interviewer didn't even blink! But you know what? I felt sorry for him, in that he couldn't or wouldn't *at least* remember the many times he was on my lap being read to as a child, being taught to read and write, being listened to and encouraged to help others, to study and seek higher education or the deep discussions he had with his father over many, many books and movies, especially on their long-distance runs and adventures. It has made me question the stories other people tell about their childhood or when I read so-called *memoirs,* even those described as *fictionalized.* It has made me wonder what students are being taught in schools…is it to avoid responsibility and to blame others or to create drama for their lives? Thus, with some wide-awake righteous anger, along with tears on my computer keyboard, I have determined to set the record straight before I am too old. I write this book to all estranged parents - everywhere. It is a basic primer. It's my 101 look at the issues of estrangement by adult children toward parents; with the hope of recovery, survival, peace and healing.

We all have our filtered memories, but they're best explored for insight and self-correction, not as justification for hurting others and especially not in the name of "truth-telling". Initially, we would confront our son about spoken or written distortions, but it only added fuel to his displaced anger toward us. He is well educated and intellectual, but often negative toward many people he has met during the course of his life. So, we pray for his heart to soften. We believe that deep down he has a good heart. Like many parents in our situation, we have tried everything possible to change our relationship with him: letters, cards, gifts, apologies **for whatever**, but he used a bad parent platform to surround himself with supporters, to write and sell books, do book readings, radio programs and television. My only comment is to, frequently, say out loud, "Help Me Jesus"!

Estrangement is often started by a sort of self-induced *filter* of many defense mechanisms about past mistakes by everyone in the drama. As in any memory, strong feelings may add more significance to an event, even some seemingly minor event. A parent may interpret something as a minor incident, but can be remembered forever by some children, and vise-versa. This memory can take on a life of its own with stories and excuses that are embedded in the travails of the brains' synapses leading to deep ruts of revised or reflective memories, real or exaggerated. Some family members stay stranded in certain decades or time periods, or even on certain political issues and they never move forward. Some may repeat the same worn-out stories that, by now, they firmly believe. Yes, sometimes estrangement is due to less than perfect parenting, or to outside forces (drugs, alcohol, mental illness), to shame, guilt, or bad decisions of selfishness. Examples may be evident when we hear about parents abandoning or abusing their children or when adult children are addicted and abuse their parents. But mostly estrangement is a choice. It is made by the adult child to disengage emotionally and physically from a relationship with a parent or other family members. **It's a choice.** It offers some sort of psychological *safe space, in a corner of the mind with a feigned apathy,* which becomes increasingly difficult to crawl out of…and crawl is what must be done… for all of us. If we cross those created boundaries of estrangement, it takes crawling out from under pride with humility, empathy, forgiveness and God's grace. Only if those boundaries of pride are crossed, can the parable of the prodigal son change the script and His grace abound.

Other than actual illness or the death of a child, estrangement from an adult child is the most painful arrow in the heart for parents. It creates an active bleeding and then a slow drip wound that doesn't go away. It is a rejection, a grief, that can't be described, only felt and anyone who helps or enables the process is contributing to that pain. Grief cannot and should not be ranked. The loss of a child, by any means is the loss of a child. It can be band-aided, but without the medicine of acknowledgement, empathy, forgiveness and grace, it never heals. To reconcile, old issues do not have to be rehashed but all parties should try to agree to "let-go," of this *living death* but that also means behaviors must change. Not just words.

When others ask normal questions, like *"How's your son?"* or *"Have you heard from your daughter?"* estranged parents come up with responses like, *"It's complicated."* or *"We don't get to see him/her much."* Then we often see the questioners' downward glances intimating such comments as, *"Wonder what they did wrong to their child?"* Then, parents tend to blame themselves even more. It is like a death without a funeral because no one really wants to hear about constant parental pain. You can't blame them. Mostly, other people just pretend your adult child doesn't exist, they don't ask or want to hear.

The problem of estrangement is growing and sometimes even encouraged by professionals, media programs, self-help and trendy groups. Adult children are encouraged to "get more space" from parents; to blame their parents or childhood for their own poor choices; to explore their own needs over others and sadly, not to worry about senior parents as they age or become ill. Self-absorption is often rewarded in our social media age. Certainly, parents can't be emotionally dependent on their children, but they do have the right to expect friendship, respect and to have boundaries from mistreatment.

Estrangement started increasing as families were ripped apart by changes in societal norms or as parents were ridiculed on television and in the movies. In fact, currently parents are often portrayed as dummies, bigots, and uncool as family traditions or morals are mocked. Instead of adult children, siblings, parents, cousins…being encouraged to talk, maybe even argue, **through** a problem or issue, with help if needed, people are often encouraged not to rock the boat, to disengage, estrange, or 'ghost' family members (ignore or pretend someone doesn't exist) or even gaslight (manipulate and deny events).

Consequently, problems never get resolved. Possibly estranged children realize they have hurt their parents, feel shame or guilt, and then withdraw, instead of working through issues or apologizing. We also see parents who enable abusive adult children because they are so fearful of being estranged by them. These parents often develop physical and psychological illnesses. They are hurt constantly by their "bullying" adult children and ride the roller coaster of pain with them. They often begin to protect their own hearts by distancing themselves from their children. They never put up real boundaries because they are emotionally blackmailed by the potential loss of grandchildren or being left alone. Estrangement excuses are bountiful. Parents are blamed for every problem or labeled "toxic." Other family members may listen, gossip and even offer encouragement to the estranged child, never once confronting them to say, *"You know what? I know your parents. Your mother and father are pretty good folks."* Thus, the problem grows and the gulf between parent and child becomes wider as time marches on. The bridge that is needed is washed away by tears.

And then, suddenly, you wake up and realize that, as parents, to survive and trust others again you have effectively *estranged* from your adult child. The difference, though, is empathy. Your door is still open, albeit with a weak chain-lock on it. Before you open it wide with trust again, something will have to change.

You haven't cut the adult child off and you want them to have peace and love, however you now have "let go" of trying. You no longer find yourself constantly reaching out or waiting for a **real** phone call from them just to check on you or to hear your voice. You stop desperately **wanting**

them to want to talk with you! You then realize that you just want to hear **their** voice…however, it is with the understanding that **they don't want to hear yours**. You recognize that, all along, you believed in reconciliation through your own filtered memories of love.

As all parents do, we only want the best for our son and we must let go, pray and hope he finds some moments of gratefulness for our parenting. We will always be his parents and will love him. That can't be erased.

CHAPTER ONE
PERSONAL REFLECTIONS

Briefly describe your own story of estrangement. If you have a partner/spouse, it helps for each of you to write out your own version of events and then discuss your respective experiences. Try to create a summary of what you have been through (you can do this now or later). One caveat: try not to blame each other, just describe your story.

CHAPTER TWO

When the Threads are Being Cut

Families impact each member differently. Each family has its' own set of dynamics, some healthy and some not so. As members struggle for love, attention, power, connection and status, all the while growing and changing as an individual, is it no wonder that the term "dysfunctional" has become the umbrella term used most to define families. Throw in some cultural, media and social media influences and it becomes a family-sized bucket of crabs with each one trying to jump out of the bucket or pull others back inside.

In the millennial age, we are facing changing realities as never before. The normal breaking-away adolescent and post-adolescent behavior may evolve into extended, contentious periods of serious adjustment. Parents who sacrifice and over-work to raise and promote their children are often shockingly surprised that their adult child not only doesn't appreciate the effort, but also may not recall those actions as benevolent, but rather as expected. They may feel entitled to anything and expect more of what parents have provided. On the flip side, many parents live vicariously through their children, suffocating them with their own goals and needs.

Additionally, society no longer has only typical nuclear families (mom, dad, traditional structure) but several others are common (not an all-inclusive list):

1) Nuclear family
2) Single Parent
3) Step or Blended Family
4) Couple only (no children in the home)
5) Grandparent Family
6) Extended Family (numerous relatives)
7) Same Gender Parents

Each type family presents challenges and benefits, i.e. couples usually have more money without children or family issues may have many more challenges and opinions with numerous relatives!

In each type family there are stereotypes and expectations, some founded and some not. For instance, a stepfamily is often thought to be difficult or disruptive, while a nuclear family may appear to be ideal. As discussions are held about estrangement, rather than the type of family being a marker, I have found that it is usually exacerbated when expectations do not become reality! The only avenue that may help to bridge the gap with estrangement is more honest, two-way communication, however, as the threads of the parent-child bond are being cut through estrangement, communication becomes less and less. Thus, expectations become enlarged on both sides, with more hurt attached and the separation realities become clearer.

EXPECTATIONS + COMMUNICATION = BETTER REALITY

All group relationships struggle for attention. They often have difficulties. Groups usually don't see issues when in the moment and it becomes shadowy to recognize the potential problems ahead. Of course, all of life is like that. It's when we are caught in an emotional storm that traits such as insight, wisdom, restraint, etc. can be hard to detect. They seem like clouds atop a fog, hard to reach, and floating above feelings of hurt, guilt, shame and rage. If this is occurring within your own family, children, grandchildren, then understand that the tunnel vision of parental love prevents rational thinking.

As I look back on my experience (or as I see it now as slow estrangement), I realize I couldn't have seen it coming. I blamed myself for many years. *"Why did I say this?"* or *"Why didn't I say that?"* I realize now that I should also have been asking questions about the creeping disrespectful, rude or cruel remarks from our adult child too.

"Why didn't I ask more about those missed visits at Thanksgiving or Christmas?"

"Why didn't I confront the hurtful comments and digs immediately?"

"Why did I worry more about hurting my child's feelings, but sacrificed my own?"

"Why did I hide my pain to family enablers who were obviously aware of what was happening?"

"Why didn't I ask for more honest discussions about his feelings and behaviors and what I was seeing with my own eyes?"

"Why didn't we get help, early on, before the gulf became so wide?"

As the topic of estrangement is becoming more prevalent, we can see that the traits of oblivion, or some would say denial, are very common. The desire is so great to have the perfect, intact family that the signs of *threads being cut* are not recognized. In fact, most of the parents say they would talk themselves out of what they were experiencing because it seemed so aberrant. Sadly, more recently, now there are therapists and self-help gurus on the internet who design methods and steps on *'How to Estrange from Family'*, which seems like an oxymoron to therapy itself. Where is one supposed to learn how to deal *with* issues and not run from them? The stories of parents who have been *estranged* by their adult children are heartbreaking.

Sometimes they are relatively young parents, and, in fact, we are hearing emerging stories of newly married young couples putting restrictions on spouses with regards to having relationships with parents. Some couples lay down rigid rules and regulations about everything, but most noticeably: visits, holiday schedules, grandchildren, traditions, religious occasions and even discussion topics. Unfortunately, some spouses relinquish to the complainer and comply. Sadly, this often extends potential estrangement restrictions to grandchildren and the pain is multiplied. All, of which can drip, drip, drip into full blown estrangement.

One vivid story was a young couple who gave written instructions to the husbands' parents on what foods *they* couldn't eat if they wanted to be around their grandchild. And it wasn't due to a peanut allergy. It was for vegetarian purposes. The spouse claimed the meat would permeate their skin and hurt their child. No amount of reason could convince her, thus the parents tried to stop eating meat. Of course, that wasn't enough. This woman would check their house and garbage for meat wrappers. Another story was of a second wife to a family who gave personality tests to family members prior to the wedding. She claimed it was to "get to know them". Then, as she communicated with them, she would tell people what their "type" was or use it against them. These are crazy examples, but they prove how one person can enter and change a whole family's dynamic. Sadly, people comply with these type of extreme control measures, which only set up for future "rules," that if broken…watch out!

Far too often we hear of an adult child who has estranged, from parents in the last season of their lives. Some estranged parents describe how they had terminal diseases and phoned their heartless Estranged Adult Child (EAC) only to be told "have someone call back when there's a death." It's easy to say those EAC's are heartless, but it's more as if they are stone-hearted. To have a heart of stone is often called hard-hearted, which is defined as incapable of being moved to pity or tenderness, unfeeling. It is as if they lost the empathy gene. Sounds kind of sociopathic, but it's often a person who has been desensitized to their own feelings and may have chosen to be unfeeling, unmerciful and insensitive. In families, it is often assumed that 'hurting people, hurt people' and that 'someone' made the person that way. In some cases that may be true, but often it's not. A past hurt can be actual, exaggerated, self-inflicted, rationalized or made-up. Sometimes people exaggerate situations to give reason or emphasis to events or feelings they do not understand. Sometimes situations are exaggerated to justify reactions or bad choices. However, to sort through family experiences and then "decide" to estrange from parents is not healthy for anyone, including the adult child making the decision. Even in the worst situations, an adult child could be kind from a distance, which helps if there is a disease or death situation. Estrangement is a choice that becomes a glue that keeps a person stuck in time and may paint them into a corner of self-inflicted misery. It then becomes a power struggle for control and is as if the toddlers have put themselves into a corner for punishment. The struggle can often lead to a full-blown temper tantrum, with hateful and hurtful words said and actions taken, from both sides of the estrangement.

The "WHY'S" of estrangement toward parents by adult children are as varied as the people who choose the behavior. But some generalities can be made. In an Australian study, in 2014, it was found that some factors were divorce, third-party alienation and multiple family stressors as contributors.

Sometimes in divorce situations one parent will "poison the well" for the children or family members with accusations and falsehoods about the other parent, thereby creating major retaliation behavior toward the accused parent. Sometimes, there are real and painful issues between the parents, however, the children get caught in the crossfire and take sides to keep peace. Often the accusations are in-the-moment statements of anger, or situations used to gain custody or more money in a divorce, yet they become larger than life stronghold statements that all parties hold onto. Many families pass on wild stories that have been exaggerated and become passed on in family legends without merit or fact. Sadly, people's reputations become damaged, many never recover, which shows how powerful words are.

Sometimes in third-party alienation, it is a daughter-in-law or son-in-law promoting discord and distortions, thus the adult child will choose sides and estrange from the parent, often to keep peace. Usually promoters of alienation have a history of doing this and become adept at the behavior. It is well known that, unless there is actual abuse or threats, no one can make a spouse do this without some complicity. Third-party alienation can also be perpetuated by aunts, uncles, in-laws, cousins, etc. It is seen when parties use their own selfish motives or agendas to enable estrangement behavior toward parents. However, it is important to remember that estranging is still a choice of the adult child.

"The LORD detests those whose hearts are perverse, but he delights in those whose ways are blameless…"
Proverbs 11:20

In multiple family stressor situations, estrangement can be a method of not dealing with matters of addiction, mental illnesses, economic strife or even legal/criminal issues. This can be on both sides of the equation and sometimes it exists for a certain period of time. Often adult children who estrange are involved in addictive behaviors and feel ashamed, thus they have no contact with family. Sometimes they are participating in a recovery program, but it could also be that in order to continue their addictive behavior they choose to have no one in their circle who might try to confront, intervene or stop their problems. If the parents have overprovided for the adult child in the past and finally stopped their enabling behaviors, it is not unusual to be cut off by the adult child.

On the parental side, if the parent is in a bad place (jobless, homeless, addicted, incarcerated or hospitalized) sometimes adult children will pull away temporarily or permanently. In our culture, today, adult children are often encouraged to have no contact with parents with problems. While becoming enmeshed in the parents' problems may be ill advised, understanding and support is merciful, historical and Biblical. In earlier days families helped each other through thick and thin. It becomes extremely painful when a parent does improve and requests contact and perhaps even asks for mercy and forgiveness only to be rejected. Sometimes this behavior is all about punishment of the parent. These types of stories are often portrayed in the media, even in celebrity families, which adds to the cultural phenomena and growth of estrangement. Blocking out parents is rampant in movie and television storylines and, in fact, in some of the scripts, audiences would think that adult children just appeared on earth with no parents. The stories only show parents as dumb or abusive. Is it no wonder that our culture promotes estrangement?

Mainly with most estrangements, whatever the stated reasons, rather than working through the issues, the adult children choose to 1) pull away, feeling this to be a lesser threat to their own feelings 2) stop contact or reduce emotional interactions for a period of time in a form of power struggle with parents 3) use estrangement as a tool to punish parents for what they perceived as rejection or past hurts or 4) have their own personal issues.

When an adult child is actively trying to maintain distance with a parent, essentially to control the relationship, that is effectively an estrangement. What is becoming clearer, as people talk more openly about the issue, is that estrangement usually happens over time. It is usually not a one-time, major incident or huge eruption that precipitates it; it is more often a festering wound that eventually succumbs to a systemic infection. Perhaps as more parents are aware of the problem and as more brave parents speak out about it, the problem will be identified earlier in the relationship and be reconciled. However, my experience with others is that most parents spend years in denial that it is even happening, as it is difficult to identify initially. When the cruel reality sets in, the gulf may seem to be too wide. Tragically, estrangement is a build-up of hurts that spill over a dam...and for the parents?? They may drown. One of the most difficult and unfair situations is that family and friends often blame the parents for the adult child's estrangement and often ask, "What happened?" "What did you do?" In general: it's the classic blame the victim scenario.

"Whoever brings ruin on their family will inherit only wind, and the fool will be servant to the wise." Proverbs 11:29

CHAPTER TWO
PERSONAL REFLECTIONS

Can you briefly describe your family type? What "WHY" questions do you ask yourself about your estrangement? (Remember we all have questions and we certainly could have handled some parenting situations better, but we never opted for estrangement. We never thought the culture would encourage cutting off parents).

CHAPTER THREE

Stages of Estrangement

The Ten "D's" = Estrangement Valley

Every single circumstance is different with the issue of estrangement. Besides parents and siblings, other family members are also affected, especially if the adult child is friends with some family members and not others.

However, what is very noticeable is how similar the reactions are by the parents. For parents, it feels like an earthquake, first denied in the beginning, but then it never stops shaking as the walls, doors, sidewalks and trees crack and all fall down. It is uncontrollable, yet the human evidence left behind is usually invisible to others. Parents hide their feelings. The adult child also becomes invisible, as he/she then disappears.

We can call the stages of this painful estrangement valley, The Ten D's. At any phase, anxiety and crisis can occur and an experienced counselor; spiritual advisor or strong friend is most helpful. If the emotional pain, grief and depression becomes deeper and immobilizing, professional help is recommended.

Denial

This can be a timeframe of seeing and experiencing separation periods with no explanations. In our family, we connected with family events and fun, but generally it was always initiated by us, the parents. We always made excuses for our son's behavior. For instance, in our son's first marriage he was enthralled by his girlfriends' parents and in fact, they helped them set up a small wedding in their home. We very much wanted to go, but we were already walking on eggshells with being accepted by them. Still, we gingerly asked to be included. Reluctantly and with rolled eyes, we were invited. Needless to say, it was uncomfortable, however we made the best of it and over-compensated with money and gifts for their honeymoon. Her family was viewed by him as "cool" while we were, well, we were not! All the while, we didn't face the way we felt and made excuses about any mistreatment. We made many mistakes, in general, during our initial period of conflict. It became easy to use denial as a defense mechanism for what we were seeing right before our own eyes.

Defensive

As time progressed, any disagreements or even mild issues, became defended positions. By all parties. In some families, full blown arguments occur (which may be healthier) however, in many families, it is mostly picky, prickly and snarky passive-aggressive communications highlighting situations which lead to hurt feelings with built-up stories defending everyone's positions. This is especially seen in in-law situations. As adult children pull away, the influence of a spouse or other family member can easily stir-up trouble in a witches' brew, of sorts, which slowly poisons the family well. For example, estranged parents describe leaving a seemingly nice family holiday visit to be met with phone calls later of accusations from an adult son or daughter over some remark said to their spouse. It is often a defensive spouse who spreads the paint of doubt that starts to strain the relationship. However, it is critical to not blame it all on the spouse, as the son or daughter makes individual choices to push parents away.

Debate

This period is often filled with "ah-ha" moments. Sadly, it may be when the situation is becoming more pronounced and the lack of contact is setting in. Many parents try really,

really, hard and over-explain, as well as ask for clarification from the adult child. "Why can't you come over to the house?" "Why weren't we invited to the party, but other family was welcomed?" "Why aren't you answering my calls/texts?" "Why are we blocked on social media?" In a painful moment for us, we were attending a huge, beautiful family wedding years ago. We were 'magically' thinking that perhaps it could be a time of healing, as we knew our son and his wife would be there. They ignored us during the wedding and, of course, didn't sit with us. However, our hope sprang eternal and we thought the reception could relax or change the situation. Well, it did all right! As we tried to sit by them to talk, some enablers garnered their attention. Calling out their names, we heard "We saved you seats, Come sit with us". We were left standing on the dance floor as they reveled with the others. Naturally, we felt foolish, but also began to see how far the disconnection was going. Other estranged parents describe similar encounters. If debating or asking questions, ideally real dialogue should be attempted, and the rift can be mended. Our experience contained no verbal communication, just hurtful e-mails or intermittent estrangement and silence. We also heard back channel, passive-aggressive type communication from others. If answers are given to any "Why" questions, they may be filled with examples of a real situation, but usually it's a misinterpreted description of a situation with a spouse, old hurts from growing up or some completely made up memory that drops your jaw. Whatever it is, can and usually does evoke hurtful words, over explaining, proof-finding (bringing up dates and trying to validate memories or throwing out facts to refute the accusations or stories) and often it involves arguing, blaming, yelling, cussing, etc. and then finality statements, i.e. "Don't ever call me again." "I hate you." "I never liked you." "You ruined my life." Some parents have been told, "I wish you were dead." Or "I can't wait until you die." You can see how the Debate period can escalate, degenerate and/or close the door. Sometimes, for some people, it also progresses in a positive way.

Distancing

The Distancing period occurs on both sides. Actual adult child estrangement usually begins with the adult child distancing from parents. It can happen in a subtle way…fewer phone calls, visits, texts and then progress to being blocked on social media or receiving e-mails that state "Give me space," or "Don't contact me for a few years." This is what we were told. In the beginning, as parents, it may seem like a phase of excessive separation or maturation to adulthood and not be taken seriously, however, if coupled with other behaviors, such as angry e-mails or texts, it is more serious.

Social media blocking has become a "ghosting" tool to erase or distance from parents and family, but it's more painful for estranged parents because usually people within a family or friends' circle *are* allowed to be part of the adult child's world. Thus, it's not unusual to hear comments dropped to hurting parents, such as: "I saw a picture of your son on Facebook and he looks great." Or "I heard your daughter is pregnant and having a little girl." Or "I saw your son was is in the hospital. Is everything okay?" and the tragedy for grandparents, "I saw your new grandchildren started school. Are you going to visit them?" Adult estranged children almost universally refuse to let grandparents see their grandchildren. Often parents 'accidentally' see pictures on social media.

Stories abound of grandparents sending gifts to grandchildren (if they even know where they live) only to have them returned or receiving notice that they were thrown away. Some grandparents save boxes of unopened gifts for a hopeful day to present to their grandchildren. It is beyond cruel, as the children miss out on that special grandparent love. Additionally, it teaches children to throw away family, thus re-creating the cycle of estrangement.

During the early phases of Distancing, it is common for parents to dream of reunion, attempt to contact, research methods to unravel the hurts and even drive by houses or work sites to 'accidentally' see or bump into to the adult child. There are reports of parents being accused of stalking. It may look like that sometimes, but it is such a desperate period that it is understandable in some ways.

Everyone must decide what is best for them, but in general, the results of seeking behavior are fruitless and may cause more animosity from the child. In our case, we were accused of being manipulative. Our daughter-in law-texted "I'm sure it must be hard for you not to see your son, but I'm not getting involved." Very cold, especially since we helped her reconcile with her own father for her wedding. It was also sad because we like her. Yet when we examined it further, we remembered she stated that she had estranged from her paternal grandparents, so we realized cutting people off felt, perhaps, like normal behavior. Thus,

Distancing is a "push-pull" period, with attempts to go forward that usually result in pulling apart.

Disillusionment

This period is noticeable when expectations bump headlong into reality. The feeling of disappointment is overwhelming and much like receiving a terrible diagnosis. It is as if the bottom fell out from under your feet and you landed on something unrecognizable. One father told me that it was as if everything he ever worked for or stood for with his estranged daughter was now a dream that had just been cancelled out. He said, "It must be like getting dementia or Alzheimer's Disease, because I'm not remembering anything I thought was there anymore." It sounds strange, but what he meant was that his relationship with his child (good times and bad and valid) was now described as worthless or inconsequential. The logical response to that feeling could be: "So who raised you my child?" or "Then, why did I bother?" In the early days for us, I remember a sibling of mine minimizing my sons' neglectful treatment of me, so I started telling people, jokingly, that "Yes, I have a grown son, but he was raised by a 'pack of wolves'." It just helped me to laugh a little. Sometimes, for me, it's difficult to remember anything good or to remember anything at all. I have prayed and texted with parents who have texted their grown children and literally waited for hours staring at their phone for a response. And even if the response is negative, they will try to find one glimmer of hope in the words. When in Disillusionment, finding Hope is far away. This valley is a pit and for our family, prayer was our only lifeline.

Despair and Depression

In some ways reaching Disillusionment can lead to Despair, a complete loss or absence of hope and Depression, feelings of sadness and malaise. Depression can be difficult to pull out of and if it continues, medical help may be needed. It is especially difficult if a history of depression is indicated. For people who lack empathy it can seem like an over-reaction, but I have heard estranged parents say, "I have no reason to live anymore." Obviously, they do, however their primary role in life was thought and felt to be parenting. Being rejected by a child seems impossible to handle, as well as completely debilitating. As difficult as Disillusionment, Despair and Depression can be, they can also reveal some of the fantasies of parenting and childrearing. For some, this becomes a turning point. It is possible that the pit and emptiness of despair can be faced realistically and allow for a resurgence of hope. In the 12-Step Recovery field it is called 'hitting bottom'. However, as long as someone bounces on an imaginary bottom or has an enabler throwing unrealistic pillows at them, the bottom is never reached. Thus, the pain can last longer. With estrangement, the expectations of what we thought would be can blind us like curtains, essentially allowing us to hide. Estrangement, like any major grief, is very confusing at times, especially if the adult child throws out bones or crumbs and then pulls back into oblivion. It can be called intermittent estrangement. Pray for clear sight. Pray for a bottom to this hell. Pray for discernment. Pray for strength. Pray for the courage to surround yourself with people who can help you.

Distrust

It is hard, when disillusioned, not to extrapolate this period to a "forever" feeling and not to attach it to other people or situations. To get through it, keep reminding yourself. This. Is. Temporary. It may last a long time, but your feelings will change. Nevertheless, it is especially difficult when the estranged adult child has contact and good times with other family members and rejects the parent or a sibling. The pain almost feels paranoid, however, if analyzed logically there is an actual and real disconnection to the parent and an actual and real connection to the others. So, it would be 'normal' to feel distrustful. Parents describe it like trying to put together a puzzle, but the puzzle pieces are withheld or hidden from the parents. Sometimes other family members or enablers will collude with the estranged child and stir the pot or spread gossip. This almost always manages to get back to the parents, thus fueling the pain. It is especially difficult when this type of attack is spread through social media. Many parents have reported untruths being posted about them. In our case, our son wrote a fictional book about a boy and girl having a horrible childhood, but he used recognizable names, settings and initially our picture for his book cover! His sister was in the picture too, which really hurt her. (His editor realized the mistake and replaced the book cover, but the damage had been done). Our daughter is an amazing, smart and strong woman who faces reality head-on, but her heart was also cracked during this time period. She missed her brother. The book issue was complicated (and confusing enough) to confront because it was written as fiction, but with all the estrangement behaviors plus his hurtful words to others and us at the time, it seemed clear that he wanted to hurt and destroy us. Which he almost did. His anger was very personal. In fact, his in-law participated in the potential destruction with an online book review that made his written words seem actually real. Sadly, we were facing a critical period in our marriage also. I am totally amazed that we managed to live through all the drama and hurt.

I now say we are in a small but growing club of parents with adult children who have said and written hurtful words about them, but like Nancy Reagan did, we will always leave the door open and the light on for our son. The difference now is that we won't allow disrespect or hurt beyond our threshold anymore.

Disconnection

Disconnection represents a time when isolation from others can become damaging and lead to more emotional pain. People who were thought to be supporters can emerge as traitors or enablers, leading to more disillusion. Critical words and questions from others may feel like arrows, so put your armor on. The opposite is true, as important people may emerge who are supporters. In our situation, a woman I did not know was sitting in front of us at church one day. This was right after the book publishing drama with our son. I heard her talking to someone else about being estranged from her own adult child. She was very sad. I took a risk and said: "I have that also". We both believe God put us together. We have been friends and supporters through many ups and downs with estrangement. She is an angel.

Disconnecting is not just about separating from those who may not be in your best interest. It's about realizing your adult child has disconnected from you for however long. Perhaps for your own survival, you may need to disconnect in a benign way from him or her as well. It may feel like betrayal or a "tit for tat" reaction - because after all, the same behavior is being applied by you. Your disconnection is not being done for malice or lack of empathy. It's most probably because you over-empathized with your child for far too long and now realize that you deserve to survive. It is the season to empathize with yourself.

If you disconnect from family and friends who add to the estrangement drama, try to do it in healthy ways versus the method your child chose to estrange from you. If you feel strong enough, tell the truth! It's that simple. Just be prepared, people may not want to listen to your truths.

Disclose and be Different

For a long while we avoided (hid from) the topic of children or family. We also avoided family situations where people might ask questions or want to discuss interactions with our son. Within family functions, we would stay away because we never knew if he would show up and snub us. It was too painful to consider the possibility. We would cringe when meeting people who would ask "How many children do you have?" Or "Where does your son live?" We have talked to parents who only claim the child or children they are connected to. It took a while, but I have found that kindness and truth has been the way for us to move forward. Our son even went through some funny estrangement periods (*looking back now it's funny*) of not calling us Mom or Dad. The infrequent contact we received was treated as a gift of crumbs from him and he would address us by our first names or initials. He did that when talking or e-mailing other people and, for a while, I was confused and eager for ANY contact, so I would answer using our first names also, not Mom or Dad. I finally realized, "Hey, wait a minute, I am his Mother. I was 16 years old and carried his 8lb, 4oz body in my little five-foot frame. I birthed him and loved him beyond, beyond as my first child. I cuddled him, read books to him, played with him, taught him about science, service, and people. His Father loved him, taught him about nature, sports, ran track with him, discussed movies, books and philosophy, worked many jobs to support him, etc. We finally stopped playing the first name game. Now, with others, we disclose and talk about estrangement, if appropriate. Usually, though, we don't go into much detail, but we don't pretend either. He can call us 'Frick and Frack,' but we only sign-off or call ourselves Mom and Dad. That is who we are.

It is hurtful when no one mentions him and, for a while, we were happy that we didn't have to respond. But now, if someone asks about our children or asks about what he is doing, we are truthful. Depending on who it is, we usually say: "He seems to be doing fine as far as we know. We don't hear much from him. He is a professor and a writer, and we hear he is happy." If people probe, because some of our story is fairly public, we may say, "He doesn't seem to want to connect much right now. Maybe someday, but we pray for his peace, his wife's…and ours too!"

We avoid back and forth wording such as, "he said or did this, and we said or did that." Nothing fruitful seems to come from it and no one really cares to hear those conversations anyway. We also need to move on from past words and mistakes, as does he.

Should someone have an issue with estrangement, we will disclose some of our experiences, not to exchange "war stories," but to validate our pain and to share potential help. And from this valley, we have moved into becoming Different. How could one not? Our reality is not dependent on our connection to our son, our estranged adult child. We don't cry and mourn daily at the lack of a deeper relationship. We don't look for ways to connect with him. Do we miss not having someone who can laugh and share history with us? With his sister and her children? Do we think of him when a memory surfaces from a thought, book, place, or song? Do we think of experiences not shared over the last many years? Do we wish he would go to dinner or a sporting event with us, especially when we see him laughing and posing with other family members? Do we remember the hilarious and fun times we had? Do we wonder what the future will hold as we age, having a son who never checks on us or asks how we are doing? YES! But, not 24/7 anymore (and it used to be). We can get through a movie now without crying, or see a father and son playing golf, or a mom comforting her child at a park. We also enjoy being with our daughter, who has positive memories of us, and seeing our grandchildren and now great grandchildren. We are so grateful for all of them.

Estrangement is truly a grief process, but of a different type. It is predominantly a cycle of grief without an ending. It is a *rejection-death*, *a living death*. It is a descent into Hell that leaves permanent burn scars. Even if there is a reconnection, the adult child may still try to retain control of the relationship with infrequent contact, measured communications, or minimal sharing - in other words…no real relationship. Sadly, parents may be so hungry for any contact, any crumb of communication, that they may put up with abusive type treatment. Stories abound from parents declaring this type of treatment.

Based on stories about the patterns of estrangement, next is a model designed to demonstrate the stages. Everyone has a unique family and a picture of their own experiences. However, this model encapsulates some of the major situations and may help you to find your stage in an Estrangement Grief Process.

FAMILY SYSTEM

ESTRANGEMENT GRIEF MODEL (COPYRIGHT © 2019-Helton)
(Real or Perceived Events Happen and Flight or Fight Begins)

 ADULT CHILD
Confusion, Anger, Blame Parent

 PARENT(S)
Confusion, Minimize, Defend

1. **VERBAL or PHYSICAL REMOVAL**
    QUESTIONS?
    Abusive to Parent, Gossips, Blocks Parent

 SHOCK,
Reach-Out, Attempt to Clarify Issues

2   **CONTROLS CONTACT**
    SHAME
    Minimal/No response, Rationalizes
    'Punishes Parents', Re-defines History

 BARGAINING,
Overexplaining, Guilt, Isolating,
Pleading, Depressed, ANGER

3   **LIVING W/O PARENTS**   ....   **REALITY SETS IN**

Goes minimal or no-contact; 'Ghosts'   Gaining Insight; Validate Parenting;
Parents; Finds Enablers; <u>No relationship</u>   Move Forward; Stop Blaming Self;
With Parents; Estrangement Gulf widens.   Get spiritual insight & Leave 'Door
Open'

Adult Child	Parent (s)
Some never change	Find Meaning in Life
Some go back & forth	Seek Support
Some reconnect	Remain Hopeful , <u>or</u>
	Live with Regret/Pain

 Sometimes Reconnect

CHAPTER THREE
PERSONAL REFLECTIONS

Where Are you in the Valley of Estrangement? Are you still in Denial? Are you still Debating issues? Are you rehashing the past trying to figure out who was right or wrong? Maybe you are Distrusting everyone or perhaps, you're ready to be Different. Take some time to describe your feelings about the Stages you have been through, even if they change daily. Add your own thoughts and stages.

CHAPTER FOUR
Placed in the Estrangement Box

Can the gulf of estrangement - the lost time, the stories told, the tears shed, ever be bridged? Most parents want their family together. Period. We want our children to live, grow and flourish like a flower box of beautiful flowers we don't ever want to pick!

The expectations of celebrations with adult children, grandchildren, in-laws and others are seared into the souls of parents. Adult children provide protection and history for parents as well as lineage, even without grandchildren. And with grandchildren, the connections become two-fold as those children need the wisdom, fun, and joy grandparents can provide. Literature, movies, theatre, community and schools are still permeated with grandparent references and experiences. So, even if estranged adult children work hard to wipe out their own parents, their children will know that somewhere there is another layer of genealogy being withheld from them. It's fascinating how people are profusely encouraged by media to do DNA ancestry testing. We especially see young adults gleefully providing testimony about their long-lost percentage of this or that heritage, when possibly there is a set of parents, grand or great-grandparents close by waiting for a phone call, visit and a hug. And they don't even need a test kit to connect!

In many ways, it seemed to us that the back and forth disconnections we had with our son was always our fault. We would retroactively examine every encounter and perseverate over how we asked or answered questions, how we listened or didn't listen, what our facial expressions were like or if we talked too much or not enough. In other words, we were jumping in and out of a box that we created, but we were like a Jack-In-Box that our son controlled with a turnkey.

The more we tried, the more control we gave to him. We were letting him define what he thought we were or had done as parents, which empowered him to be more emotionally abusive to us. We enveloped him with a reflection of what he thought he was - the center of the universe.

Why do we, as parents, feel we must build the bridge to reconciliation? If someone, other than our child, hurt us deeply and abused us emotionally, would we try to build a bridge to them? Should we? Of course not, unless we are masochistic. Can we get out of the estrangement box? Who

put us in the box? It seems, with our children, we continue

to default back and forth, thinking estrangement is:

1. All our fault
2. We need to fix it
3. We can fix it
4. We must make amends (over and over)
5. Repeat

And repeat we do.

Story after story of broken hearted, estranged parents

describe efforts to reunite with estranged children. It reminds

me of an incident my husband told about once of when he

saw a starving, scared, stray momma dog on the streets. He

could tell she needed help, so he tried to catch her, but it

made her more scared and wary. She was determined to stay

away. He followed her and she ran more. Knowing she was

hungry, he decided to get her food. He went into a corner

store and bought a pack of hot dogs. He then started running

after her with the hot dogs and she ran faster, so he started

throwing the hot dogs ahead of her, hoping she would stop

to eat. Eventually, he stopped and realized that the more he pursued, the more she would flee. He finally set the hot dogs down and walked away. If she wanted them, she would stop and find them. Sometimes it's best to lay down the hot dogs.

Other people help to lift us into the box of estrangement. We may already feel like we are in the box, but others can add to this, if we allow it. Usually, when others enable or perpetuate estrangement, it is for their own edification. In other words, it is done in some way to benefit them, to meet their own needs, instead of as it should be in the Romans 15:2 sense, *"Each of us is to please his neighbor for his good, to his edification."*

Instead, the edification is done to improve the enabler or spouse in some way. It is probable they don't realize the extent of their behavior due to being blinded by the desire to meet their own needs. Some examples:

1. The enabler has a history of inability to face conflict of any kind. They may perceive all discussion as

hostile and avoid it at all costs, thus refusing to discuss differences, or question normal situations or have a difference of opinion. Thus, avoidance is perpetuated, even if it means no contact with the parent. It is easier for them to have contact with the estranged child, as they usually don't want to discuss or resolve issues either.

2. The enabler or spouse has an old beef or hidden issue with the parents. This is probably the most common situation. Some old hurt - actual or real, or projected - from some other experience with another person or some old jealous, competitive feeling has emerged within the enabler. You may not even realize it. They may not either. This feeling may fester, and at any chance, it will couple with a problem or difficult situation the parent may have. These are the types of stories that can evolve into old family feuds. However, they can also play out like a chess game

where those in control use all the players to make moves. Much mental energy and time can be wasted trying to figure out these games. It's best to walk away from the game table and let them play with each other, even if you feel like flipping the table over. It helps to pretend your mind has a file space labeled "I don't understand". When it feels as if a mental game or manipulation is occurring, just put the situation in the file. Take it out and revisit it, if needed, but over time, it may become a file that can be deleted in order to protect your heart.

3. Another reason some enablers may buy into taking sides against a parent in an estrangement situation is the complete fear that something similar could happen to them. It's typical in crime situations to 'blame the victim' in order to distance oneself from the possibility of becoming a victim. For example, a person may think, *"Well, I wouldn't have left my car*

unlocked, like she did, thus I wouldn't have been robbed". Thus, the enabler may try to get as many dirty details as possible about the estrangement, then commiserate with the estranged child, distance from the parent and thus justify that they would never have done whatever the adult child told them the parent did wrong. Of course, their own children would *never* estrange from them. It is a circuitous method of mental self-protection, perhaps some cognitive dissonance. Most people believe parents and children will always support each other and want to be together, so to hear about estrangement is inconsistent with a prevailing belief. Something must be explained or created to remove the feeling of dissonance.

4. Some enablers or spouses are just plain jealous of parents. It's a fact that some people can't handle seeing people happy or share in another's joy. They

live in a constant state of competition. Parents can be viewed as competitors who must be knocked off. When any small infraction in a relationship emerges, it is seen as a "feet of clay" situation and instead of helping to shore up the person, the clay is seen as an opportunity to topple them. This is experienced, often, from other family members.

5. If a parent feels like he/she is living in an estrangement box, there exists a beauty in that the box can be opened from the inside out. It may feel like hiding in the box helps, and truthfully, sometimes it does help for a while, but it is dark, lonely, scary and builds with pressure. Someone else may have prompted or shamed you to get into that box but you have the right to get out. You may need to grieve inside for a while, and you will know when that time is up. But, don't ever let someone keep you there. Bust out. Go to the light and throw that box

away! Your physical, spiritual, emotional and relational health depends on it.

CHAPTER FOUR
PERSONAL REFLECTIONS

Do you feel your situation has you in a 'box'?

Are you repeating the same behaviors and not moving forward yourself?

Are there other players (enablers) in your family or friend circle who seem to be 'stirring the pot' with your estranged child and do they drain your heart also?

Do you find yourself obsessing over your estranged child and the enablers?

<u>Now, Hard Questions Here</u>: Can you describe WHY you are allowing them to live in your head and keep you in a box? Are you gaining anything from this? Avoidance? Fear? Anger? Pride? Blaming? Victimhood?

Have you placed your Estranged Child in a box? Have you labeled that box with a permanent or temporary label? Would you allow them to get out?

CHAPTER FIVE
Stress and Estrangement

When a child estranges from the parent(s) it creates a hole

in the family structure, but it is usually a hole everyone walks

around. Many people pretend the hole isn't there. Some

people know about the hole, but let others fall in it. Some

people put planks and boards over the hole to cross it and

sometimes, sometimes, the child will fill in the hole and it

disappears. Regardless of how the empty place for the

estranged child is treated, it becomes a stressor of immense proportion for the family, especially the rejected parents.

This is not to say the adult child doesn't suffer, because research shows they do, in one way or another. Pain for the child can be due to a 'lost child' void they may feel from time to time; a lack of someone who has shared history with them; lack of medical information or just from the use of the constant negative energy they use to push their own parents away. Some adult children are thought to feel nothing, having major narcissistic personalities, with lack of empathy. Perhaps the most difficult are the developed feeling of nothingness or apathy. This can happen on both sides of the equation. Parents often fall into apathy as a protective mechanism for their hearts. Dashed hopes can only be sustained for so long and every individual has his/her own limits. Prayer is especially critical in this phase, especially if the parent has no spouse, is elderly or alone. And, certainly spiritual or professional counseling is critical if depression and anxiety become an unresolved pit leading to more self-degradation or perhaps harm. Seek help and remember: You don't deserve this. You are not alone.

It's hard to know for sure who is or isn't under stress or pain from estrangement grief because the distortions from the stories of estrangement are usually biased. Rejection from both sides of the family equation is often loudly justified and each can become entrenched in their own righteous views. It is difficult to break through and usually becomes an even stronger tug-of-war.

The main phenomena to recognize about estrangement is that it causes deep grief and some form of the grieving process. It is different than other types of grieving in that it is often still a hidden and unspoken pain. Not only do many estranged parents fail to reveal what has happened, but others who know about it often treat it as a taboo or an unspoken subject. When this happens, it makes estrangement even more unspeakable and more painful for the parents. It is as if the child was murdered and they are being blamed!

Most problems in life have some form of resolution. Experiences with estranged parents demonstrate a roller coaster of trials with few successes, unless the estranged child is trying also. So, losing your child from your parental circle, and yet knowing they are out there but refusing, rejecting or minimizing your involvement, hugs, or shared information is a constant level of unresolved grief which can only cause stress and harm to the body and soul. Over time it can become a form of Post Traumatic Stress, PTSD, and cause physical, mental, emotional and spiritual harm.

GRIEF/LOSS INFORMATION

- GRIEF: deep mental anguish, as that arising from bereavement.

- LOSS: the condition of being deprived or bereaved of someone or something.

"For in much wisdom is much grief:

74

and he that increaseth knowledge increaseth sorrow."
Ecclesiastes 1:18 (KJV)

- GRIEF HURTS. It hurts physically, mentally, and spiritually. Grief and loss can also exacerbate an existing illness, lower the immune system and make us more susceptible to major health problems. Stress reactions described in early research clearly note that in the alarm phase of grief, the immediate pain or event, causes the sympathetic nervous system in the body to respond with catecholamine hormones like adrenaline.

- Chemicals are triggered in the brain and body by the hypothalamus to the pituitary gland and then the adrenal glands, which produce ACTH (adrenocorticotrophin hormone). ACTH is the "protection for battle" hormone. It causes the reaction in the adrenal glands to produce cortisol. Initially this hormone is positive. It helps us to be prepared for "fight or flight." But when stress or grief continues over time, chronic high levels of this stress hormone can remain in the blood stream, possibly affecting the immune system. Excessive cortisol is linked to chronic inflammation, damaged blood vessels, brain cells and increased risk for weight gain, colds, sleep deprivation (which also is related to memory loss), depression, ulcers, and joint problems. Unresolved grief and stress may also lead to increased alcohol or drug use, and other unhealthy behaviors. (AARP Bulletin, November 2014,

STRESS by Elizabeth Agnvall; Mary Neis & Melanie McEwen, "Community Public Health Nursing", 2011; Cortisol and Stress: How to Stay Healthy, by Elizabeth Scott, 2014)

- If you doubt that stress can seriously affect the body, recognize this fact: Extreme stress, grief, shock, or fear can cause a syndrome known as the "broken heart syndrome," clinically called *Takotsubo Cardiomyopathy*. With this syndrome, the heart literally changes shape; it morphs and balloons, causing the pumping chambers to have difficulty pumping. The shape change looks like the name of the syndrome (in Japanese the *takot subo* is an octopus pot) which is similar to the shape the heart takes on with this syndrome. In fact, this shape, with symptoms, is how the syndrome is diagnosed in a cardiac scan. This syndrome is temporary, but it needs to be diagnosed and treated as it can actually be a critical heart condition leading to heart failure. It can be triggered by extremely stressful incidents (emotional and/or physical), and the symptoms mimic a heart attack (myocardial infarction) with chest pain, shortness of breath, and interruption of the heart's pumping and rhythm. It is in reaction to the massive volume of stress hormones and listen up Moms, it occurs most often in women. (health.harvard.edu/newsletters/Harvard_womens_health_watch)

Additionally, in some family estrangement situations, elder abuse emerges, and parents are at risk for physical, emotional and financial abuse. The parents are emotionally depleted and hungry for any contact with the adult estranged child. It is not unusual for them to accept any kind of abusive treatment, give the child money or property and hide the information from other family members or authorities. Parents of adult estranged children are vulnerable to exploitation from strangers and criminals due to the isolation.

- Just think about the old phrase "scared to death" when you think about stress, grief, and loss. Consider how God designed the body to be on guard and to react to emotions, difficult situations, and danger. Then reverse that in your mind and logic should tell you that if it can go one way (to the negative) or it can go the other (toward the positive).

- You can begin to heal the grief and loss you go through, step-by-step. It's your choice. You can stay stuck in different phases, or you can work through them. The operative word is "through".

- Grief is like an infection or a boil in the body. It must be cleaned out, expressed, and healed with medicine. Otherwise, it can spread and destroy the body, mind, and spirit. Talk with a counselor if the emotional pain becomes worse.

- Let your tears flow—tears kept inside will crack the heart. Express them, let them flow; they are filled with healing salve and will water your soul.

"Blessed are they that mourn- for they shall be comforted." Matthew 5:4 (KJV)

The grief process is not linear. It usually does have defined phases, but phases that are individual and permeable—they are different for everyone, and there is no "right" or "wrong" way to grieve. When we have a major life issue or event (health, family, marriage, divorce, crime, death) and thus feel grief, loss, fear, betrayal—major changes in life—we go up and down and in and out of the phases of grief and loss. Grief issues can affect every aspect of our life and often throw us into an incomprehensible vortex of feelings.

Model of an ACTIVE GENERAL GRIEVING PROCESS MODEL (The Estrangement Model fits within this, especially the back and forth stages)

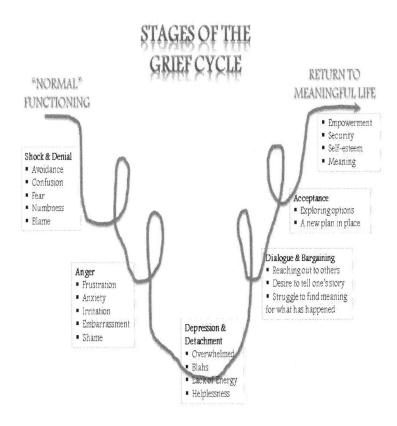

The main question about grief is: Are you mostly moving forward? The problem with the usual grieving process is found in the event.

With Estrangement, it usually takes a while to even figure out what is happening, or what the actual event is. Consequently, the shock and denial phase can be generally prolonged. We hear of parents trying for years to make sense out of the confusion and negative behavior of their adult estranged child. The anger phase also tends to be longer due to the embarrassment and shame felt by the parents. Far too many blame the parents, thus "shut down" occurs and parents do not share their feelings or hurts. Then, when reality begins to hit, despite all efforts to mend and heal the relationship, parents may hit the floor and fall into depression. Some parents remain stuck in this phase and eventually become so miserable they express an avid desire to die. This is not unusual, especially if the child is friends with other family members and no one is acknowledging or supporting the parents. Whereas, the next phase should be moving to dialoguing/bargaining, there are usually few people with whom to declare feelings, which is why opening up and talking to supportive people is so vital.

Moving forward to acceptance and a return to meaning, otherwise known as the new normal, requires active decision making and work, but it is possible. It is not that you will move beyond the estrangement facts because, if you're living in reality, they may always be there. In fact, some people may prompt you to just "move on," but all one can do is "move through" and learn. You can't forget you have a child, but you can begin to lessen the pain of rejection grief.

Working through grief and loss can bring anyone to their knees, but it can also allow a more comprehensive understanding of life and help us to empathize with others who are dealing with losses.

We know that support from others is critical when dealing with painful losses. Support group websites, books, and recovery groups, as well as spiritual connections, promote inner healing.

- Prayer, friends, counselors, support groups, ministers, priests, and rabbis can help you, especially those who have been through what you are experiencing, whatever your circumstance. But your biggest loss would occur if you were to deprive yourself of God.

- Remember: God is with us 24/7. He will walk any lonesome, dark valley with us. We are never alone.

2. *"The LORD is my shepherd; I shall not want.[2]*

3. *He maketh me to lie down in green pastures:*

4. *he leadeth me beside the still waters.[3]*

5. *He restoreth my soul:*

6. *he leadeth me in the paths of righteousness for his name's sake.[4]*

7. *Yea, though I walk through the valley of the shadow of death,*

8. *I will fear no evil: for thou art with me;*

9. *thy rod and thy staff they comfort me."*

Psalm 23:1–4 (KJV)

CHAPTER FIVE
PERSONAL REFLECTIONS

Find yourself on the Grief Model: Are you stuck? Moving forward?

Going back and forth? Do you have someone, a group, a Church or neighborhood community where you can express honestly how you feel about your specific estrangement situation? Do you feel your physical health has suffered from grieving the lost time with your child? What can you do right <u>now</u> to feel better about YOU? Take a walk? Call a hotline? Go to Church? Volunteer? Pray?

CHAPTER SIX
Tales of Woe

There are so many terrible stories in the family sagas of estrangement. Find yours. Or write yours. Unfortunately, for far too long, no one talked about this issue and parents/families have suffered in silence and shame. Many still do. When the topic is brought up, it is surprising how many people are estranged from their adult children and don't understand it. Sadly, parents start identifying themselves only as "estranged parents", which is something done to them, not who they are.

Some of the stories from estranged families describe:

The seemingly, sudden-slam-the-door-type, the drip-drip-torture type, the death-by-a-thousand-cuts type, the addiction, legal, bleed-you-dry type, the move-1,000-miles-away type, the lying-dog type, the sneaky-snake type, the rollercoaster-hope-dash-hopes type, the I'll-help-you-hate-your-parents type and the I'm-taking-you-down type. There are many others, especially when spouses and enablers get involved and stir the pot. It often becomes a throw-you-in-the-cactus- patch type of situation. It's painful and the thorns don't come out!

Without droning on with he said/she said examples, here are some categories, along with examples, of the types of estrangements we have heard about from parents. The general descriptions may help you find yourselves or your situation. Hopefully, you will see you are not alone and possibly gain more understanding about estrangement. The categories of examples are truly endless and as complicated as all people and families. A factor that has been particularly eye-opening for us is the 'off and on' aspect of some estrangements. It's difficult to know what to call the relationship when the 'prodigal child' returns home but disappears for a while again, turning an open door into a revolving door. It is equally difficult to know whether to let your guard down or not. Perhaps for the adult child it is the same, as they are filtering all the experiences respectively.

The Poisoned Well

It was the second marriage for both individuals, and each brought children to the relationship…teenagers! In the beginning the teens seemed pretty cool with their new step-dad and step-mom, after all the step-dad had a lot of stuff: money, nice car, big house, swimming pool, horses, etc. and he was a nice guy. As the days went by, friends were encouraged to visit their house and enjoy the privileges of the Dad's wealth. All seemed fine, but as divorced families do, child visitations occurred with each of the biological parents. Each time the visits happened, the teens from both sides returned with a vengeance and extreme anger and anxiety. It became clear, over time, that the ex-spouses were verbalizing negative, blaming information about the new spouse, as well as the remaining parent. So often, venomous words from an ex-spouse are embedded into an already grieving or confused child's head and to "keep peace" or fantasize a reconciliation, the child will side with the negative parent. It's especially hurtful if other family members pile on and throw gasoline on the fire. That's not to say that real issues didn't happen to break up the marriage, but drawing the child into them is unhealthy and sets a stage for estrangement. In this family, the stepchildren eventually worked through their feelings, except for one son. He pulled away totally from his biological father, sided with his divorced mother and estranged from his father and siblings.

The son was so poisoned, from years of negative remarks and actual lies about his father, that he carried the estrangement behavior into his adult life, blaming the father and serving up poisoned water to anyone who would *taste* it. Bitterness has a nasty taste and withers the heart, especially the hearts of those who embrace it.

The Son-In-Law-from-Hell (SILFH)
or Daughter-In-Law-from-Hell (DILFH)

This type of situation is mostly self-explanatory however, it often doesn't start off that way. Stories abound about initial loving relationships between the adult children, parents/in-laws and melded families. It's not uncommon for parents of an estranged child to say, "Everything was fine until after the wedding and then it wasn't." We have heard of parents who gave money, gifts, parties, cars, houses, etc. only to have the SIL or DIL turn against them after they got what they wanted. Usually, it starts with an event or contrived issue.

One example was a couple married for a few years who visited his parents in what seemed to be an amicable visit. When the couple returned home, the parents received a phone call from the son stating: "We won't ever be visiting at your home again. If we want to see you, we will let you know and meet you at a restaurant." Stunned, the mother asked, "Why? What happened?" The son was vague, but stated that his wife was "tired of not being listened to" and felt that his father was "abusive" and "didn't like the way the mother cooked or cleaned house and if they ever had children they were not going to let them be exposed to them, so they might as well end the visits!"

In other words, the DILFH had a stored sack of grievances to throw at her mother-in-law. The mother was crying on the phone by now and asking for examples of what she had done or said, to which the son added that he felt "guilted" by her crying. He agreed with his wife and hung up the phone. What followed was a myriad of painful discussions and texting for weeks, months and then years of an ever deepening "splitting" by the DILFH resulting in estrangement. By the time grandchildren arrived, the DILFH indeed kept her promise and would not allow the grandparents to see their grandchildren. Clearly, the son was complicit and allowed the behavior, however, the match that lit the fire was the DILFH. The reasons for estranging would be articulated frequently to anyone who would listen, but never truly understood, which is common and best left to experts or to prayers.

In another example a grown daughter who had met and married a charming man ended up in an abusive situation. An abusive argument was witnessed by the parents at their home which required her parents to call law enforcement for her physical protection. Once this occurred, the SILFH never stopped pulling her away from her parents in order to control and bully her. She stayed married to him. In abuse situations, defending the abuser is not uncommon and authorities must be involved for safety, however, some parents find themselves living in the horror of seeing their daughter abused, estranged and then, possibly, even moved states away, and protection becomes a nightmare of wondering.

Abuse is an added variable to estrangement and understanding the cycle of abuse is critical for the family system. If the battered spouse can realize the pattern of the abuser (tension building, abuse and honeymoon phases), perhaps she can understand that she cannot change him. The cycle not only repeats but escalates. Perhaps she will get support and move out, but unfortunately, often the woman is degraded and manipulated into believing whatever the abuser tells her. In time, the battered woman becomes like a hostage and may turn totally against her parents and family. Information and resources are available, and it is important to protect oneself from the violence of an abuser, especially with addiction problems. Learn your area resources. You may need protective orders, shelter information, children's protective services and police protection, even for yourselves. Sadly, this is sometimes not enough, and victims become statistics, including children and parents. It is not an issue to be dealt with lightly.

The "Perfect Parent" and "Perfect Family"

Well, obviously there is no such entity as a perfect family, but to hear some people describe their family or to see what is posted on social media sites, it sure appears that way at times. If parents perceive that they really are perfect, it is incredibly shocking to have an adult child estrange. In one case, there was a physician/ psychiatrist and his artistic wife who had two handsome/beautiful, healthy and smart children. By all appearances the children were given every opportunity to express their feelings, to process decisions, to achieve, to participate in sports and theatre and to engage with friends and other family members. When the daughter turned eighteen years of age and attended college, she began to isolate herself from her family. She would not return calls or participate in family events. The parents chocked it up to a normal growing process, however, they were treated with increasing disdain by the daughter. Despite buying her a car, paying for her college, trips and extra activities, the daughter would purposely not be at the university when the parents went for a visit. Additionally, she would not come home for holidays when it was evident that others in her circle of friends did. The perfect parents could not stop processing how they had literally "done everything" in the world for this daughter, including paying for her ever-demanding plastic surgery! By constantly succumbing to the daughters' requests, demands and emotional abuse, they inadvertently were giving her the power to continue.

It wasn't long before any and all mistakes or bad choices made by the daughter became the "fault" of her parents. Initially, the parents beat themselves up trying to help the daughter out of all her bad choices. This was their default, as is often for many parents. Their daughter became more distant, moved in with repeated boyfriends and lived a life without parental connections. In spite of all attempts, including paying for counseling and begging for contact, the daughter pulled further away. She eventually moved away, had a baby with a new boyfriend, blocked all contact with her parents and they still have not seen their grandchild. If the lives of the parents, along with all of the attempts to clear up the relationship were mapped out, it would appear that they did everything perfectly to repair the relationship. It's an example of why it is so hurtful when people blame parents for an adult child's hurtful choices.

Sometimes the perfect family means there was a one-sided relationship. The parents have literally done it all. The children were provided it all. The adult children thus expected it all. And the adult child dumped it all, including the parents.

Identity and Breaking Away

The internet is rampant with articles and sources on how to *break away* from parents; especially those defined as *toxic*, which has become the psycho-babble buzz word to justify estrangement. As parents, if you feel confused now, reading these references can put you under your bed. In fact, some parents of estranged adult children truly express that they wonder why in the world they ever had children.

Once again, it's true that some parents can be harmful and abusive, but the majority are not. That's just a fact. However, when describing so-called toxic parents, the categories are perilous and may give inaccurate advice to adult children, especially in our current culture of changing family structures. For instance, if parents were in any way structured and disciplined, they may be labeled as controlling or over-bearing. If the parents taught community service, spirituality or engaged in a particular religion, they may be labeled as guilting or emotionally abusive. If the parents encouraged chores or rules, they may be said not to respect the child's boundaries or even be termed as being abusive. Allow me to clarify that ALL parents could do a better job at the skill set of parenting and most wish they had, especially with all the new parenting information that is now available.

It's important to note that there is the normality of *breaking away* in adult development, but it can be done without destroying relationships within families or with parents. In fact, it is critical to 'break away' and follow ones' life story and dreams. In past generations, it was prompted often through necessity of survival, certainly as other lands were explored and developed. Most explorers probably never saw parents again, as they sailed off to new lands. Additionally, some separations were prompted by job opportunities and even wars. It was sometimes seen as the way for a young man to mature. Great literature, movies and legends grew out of those explorations. However, in most of the stories, there was always an ethos or yearning for home. It was usually the point of the adventure plot as the forever changed, hungry and grateful person returned home. In today's world, it is difficult, at best, to even note parents or homecomings, unless they are riddled with angst, revenge or ridicule.

Understanding the process of *breaking away* is important and it helps to review developmental phases of growth, which we all had to muddle through. A good information source for the stages of psycho-social development is old, but still helpful. It is from Erik Erikson and his Eight Stages in the Theory of Psychosocial Development. (1* *Childhood and Society*). It's helpful also because it puts common developmental behaviors within the context of environmental influences.

Every person develops unique characteristics and identities. The traits we display are built on psychosocial needs at different ages/stages. It is those needs that when met or unmet can lead to crisis or resolution to move us forward to the next phase. Parents or caretakers are critical to this forward development for minors, but as we grow and develop, we must also face and resolve the issues ourselves. We all went through some form of these stages and it helps us to review them as we look back on our family-of-origin issues.

Erikson's Theory of Development fits well into the issues of estrangement and may help us to examine and understand our own family, as well as our relationships with our children at different ages/stages. Additionally, it may help to refresh yourself about these stages, and to reflect on your own current stage. We never stop growing and moving through the stages of life.

The struggle with estrangement is much like living with a chronic disease. It is challenging enough to navigate the normal phases and stages of life development but when a major stressor is underlining everything, it can magnify emotions and physical issues.

For estranged parents, trying to integrate the loss of a child within a season or stage, it can feel like a whirlpool of quicksand at times. It is especially difficult when someone tells parents to move on or get over the pain. Again, each person must work through the steps of grieving family loss at their own speed. However, as estranged parents decide to heal themselves, they often look for methods and people who can help move them along through the grief. Support groups, counselors, spiritual counseling, and medical personnel may assist those who are stuck and spiraling deeper into depression or self-destruction. It's imperative to be observant concerning this behavior and refer those in this situation.

According to Erikson, common developmental stages include:

Stage One – Trust vs. Mistrust. Infant to eighteen months must have their basic level needs met to develop trust. This is manifested by food, comfort, love and bonding. This is the responsibility of the parents in order to make the child feel secure in their environment.

Stage Two – Autonomy vs. Shame and Doubt. Eighteen months to three years represents the stage where children are moving into wanting to do things on their own. This is critical to feeling accomplished and moving forward with skills, i.e. feeding self, grooming, toileting, etc., especially if other children are capable around them. Encouragement and patience are critical.

Stage Three – Initiative vs. Guilt. Three to five years are about practice and exploration. Self-esteem is built as the child is guided but learns to accomplish tasks on their own. Having to ask for help can be perceived as failing, thus parents should act more as guiding shepherds, rather than instructors, to teach children tasks.

Stage Four – Industry vs. Inferiority. Five to thirteen years is labeled the age of reason and builds as children learn more facts that relate to their environment. Usually much of this is occurring in school, but also in afterschool play and organized activities. The child gains self-awareness and wants to relate to peers, compete and perform similar tasks, leading to feelings of industry or inferiority.

Stage Five – Identity vs. Role Confusion. Thirteen to twenty-one years is usually described as the self-discovery and sexual identity period, however, in our culture today there is more exposure to sexual issues and identity may become more of a crisis period. Additionally, this is when the transition is occurring as the child enters adulthood and finds a role in society (another difficult task, especially if expectations conflict with parents).

Stage Six – Intimacy vs. Isolation. Twenty-One to-thirty-nine are the years of finding meaningful relationships and/or a mate. It can be stressful and fearful and, one would think, especially difficult if estranged from family.

Stage Seven – Generativity vs. Stagnation. Forty to sixty-five years are seen as our work/productivity years that lead to finding meaning in life and growth. That includes Parents also!

Stage Eight – Ego Integrity vs. Despair. Sixty-five years and older are the years of feeling rewarded by fulfilling significant events in ones' life, looking back and being content versus living with regrets and depression. A difficult stage if estranged from children or family.

Each of Eriksons' defined stages provide a model for realizing what is needed, in a basic sense, before someone can fruitfully move to the next phase. If many gaps occur within the different stages, it may be difficult for the developing person. In other words, one can be a 30-year-old adult and not have developed well through some earlier phases, thus some behaviors may be stunted. What is important to note in the later stages of thirteen years and up, is that much of the struggle to succeed is driven by the inner self and dependent on the environment of the child. They must push against some struggles and learn from them.

Another important note is that parents can help with many of the struggles even adult children encounter, thus pushing away from parents is not the most productive or wise behavior. As the estranged parents, again, recognize that you are in a stage also, depending on your age. You also had your own family-of-origin encounters and may have not had smooth transitions yourself, while growing up.

While we can't be emotional crutches for our adult children, how healing it is, when both parties can learn, grow, **empathize** and relate to each other. Some families have this. Estranged parents do not. Perhaps someday. Spiritual connection and Prayer are definitely anchors for us all in all the stages of life, as well as in the estrangement grief cycle.

Fractured-Split Families

It is apparent in our world today that many families can be described only as a <u>MESS</u>. What was once the easily definable family is now not always recognizable, however perhaps the vision of what we defined as "family" was merely a mirage. Either way, we see more single parents, divorced couples, blended families and creative parenting within families. In the effort to bring order to chaos, some players opt out. This goes for parents, as well as adult children. An example of this type situation was brought to our attention through a couple who had emerged from addiction problems. They each had overcome addictions, however, the collateral damage from days and nights of living addicted left their three children floundering and split away from them: living with grandparents, aunts and uncles and sometimes friends from school.

The parents conquered their addictions when the children were teenagers. They all moved back in together and assumed all would be smooth. Of course, the unintended consequences of addictions are also relegated those who are damaged around the addict. As the children grew, so did their resentment and anger. Unfortunately, this family didn't follow up with counseling. As soon as each teen turned eighteen, they moved out of the home. The teens told their parents they "needed their space" and blamed them for a lost childhood. The parental pain was defined as being filled with guilt and remorse, but to make matters worse, other family members piled on and sided with the teens, including allowing them to move into their homes. Thus, their asking for space actually became hiding from truths and not learning to work through them.

Now, obviously these teens had experienced real and harsh issues, but with meddling and enabling from others, they delayed contact with professional help and moved into full blown estrangement. Fortunately, the parents stayed sober and through counseling were able to make amends with their adult children. The time lost was enormous.

The good news is the adult children learned valuable methods of conflict resolution and worked toward a healthy relationship with their mother and father. What could have become life-long separation was turned around. Some family members continued lurking around to re-stir the pot, at times, but the adult children recognized the behavior and didn't play the game.

Sometimes, these types of family events, where sides are drawn, become generational squabbles and estrangements.

The Hatfields and the McCoys

Family feuds are everywhere. They're in the very rich, the middle and low-income families. If you think about it, it's just a tribal type of estrangement! We heard stories growing up about grandparent and great grandparent generational feuds that carried themselves forward into our little family. They would often play out when discussing weddings, party invitations or vacation visits. "We can't invite them…They don't get along with *so and so*." Then, there are blanket descriptive statements, such as: "That's' the *radical* side of the family." And that would be the end of that discussion! There are also temporary status exclamations, such as: "We can't go on a vacation and visit because so-and-so just had a fight with (fill in the blank)." Some of this is normal family lore, however, deep feuds often are passed down in families with customized descriptions: "They're the nutty ones. They're the drinkers. They're the religious clan." The list can be endless and descriptions unmerciful.

With estrangement of parents by adult children, the pattern is essentially developing a future feud just by the act of estranging. There will be time lost, feelings hurt, stories exaggerated, battle examples and scars rendered by both sides. This, of course, makes any repairs increasingly difficult. Family feuds are perilous inheritance gifts that can be passed on to children and grandchildren who are usually the pawns and victims of the drama.

We have all, at times, been guilty of participating in selective stories (gossip) about family members. I have found it very difficult for that person to ever step out from the cardboard, cut-out image created about him or her. It's as if every time a person or event is mentioned, a family index box is opened up and a scripted card is pulled out and read. Hatfield and McCoy type feuds can perpetuate estrangement and encourage both splitting and family triangles. How would any of us change or receive mercy and grace if that happened to us? And, of course it does, as the story of our own estrangement is told.

Aging Away

Some of the saddest, most horrific examples of estrangement are seen in the senior or elderly population.

Even if it's not an obvious cut-off relationship to parents by adult children, all one needs to do is visit a nursing home or senior center to see some neglected and lonely elders. Many families visit and provide support when a loved one lives in an assisted living center however, many are forgotten victims of too-busy children, materialistic cultures and financially exploited elders.

Recently we observed an older friend become increasingly frail and in need of clear help for major physical health issues. She was a vibrant, well-educated woman, working into her 70's, a professional who had lost her husband several years earlier. She had three grown children who did not live close to her. As she struggled to adjust to her grief and new role of being a widow, her health quickly deteriorated. She had never disclosed that her children had estranged from her when their father died. (Oh, the secrets we keep!) And she NEVER spoke ill of her grown children, even though it was obvious that they ignored her. When she needed more help, we had to reach out to her family and also ask her for more information. What came tumbling out was years of emotional pain and longing for her children. What came out from them were stories about their busy lives, her 'issues' and many questions about what assets she had acquired. Within a matter of months, our friend passed away and the children who could never find the time to visit or come repair her house or care for her were there in days, going through her belongings.

This example made me realize the importance of getting one's affairs in order and thinking seriously about who would be loyal and caring as we age and who should inherit any assets acquired.

Personality Disturbances

It almost seems self-evident that anyone who would estrange from their parents has a personality disturbance, but that's not necessarily so, especially in this age, when it's almost fashionable to cut off parents. It's especially difficult when alcohol or drugs are misused and terrifying when grandchildren are involved. Some of the cut off children seem lost and sad but seem not to know how to deal with the situation, or really any difficult relationship. Therapy, sometimes medication, support groups and spiritual work may be necessary to work through personality disturbances. One clear sign is the rollercoaster world of off-and-on communication and connections. When order is disrupted in a family system chaos erupts. It's a law of nature. Some people have deep seated needs to be in control or at the center of everything (narcissistic or worse). Some have life-long patterns of creating chaos and some have emotional hurts that are repeated over and over. What seems illogical in these situations often works for the person creating the chaos, however, those outside of the storm center struggle to understand a non-understandable situation. If someone cuts us off; there will be disruption and chaos and we must be the ones to re-stabilize ourselves and have healthy boundaries.

In nature, two examples of what can happen with a cut off situation are interesting. In the bee world, the Queen Mum is everything. There is no space in the colony for more than one queen. The workers, scouts and drones all surround the queen bee and the production of honey flourishes. When the hive is too large or nourishment is reduced, the worker bees are induced to create a new queen and the hive swarms. The queen is 'clipped' or 'cut off' and apparent chaos ensues, however, it's all designed to create order within the hive and to get back to business!

In human terms, families/parents bring order and the mother should be the queen, the kind who knows how and when to step laterally for a new female in the 'hive'. However, sometimes, instead of working out the new pecking order an in-law will cut off the queen in any way possible. Whereas in nature, it is a natural process, in the human world it is purposefully destructive to family order.

Another example of a cut off effect in nature is in the weather. It is called a "cut off low pressure" system. It's an interaction between warm and cold air that becomes unbalanced and becomes stuck or "cut off" due to weak steering currents. It usually begins as a trough in upper air currents and becomes cut off. Consequently, it forms a closed circulation and drifts in a displaced manner. It may remain stationary and go in an opposite direction. It tends to have deep pressure. The winds spiral and intensify. The low can bring torrential amounts of rain and storms. It is chaotic. Much like a cut off low, when our adult children cut themselves off from parents and the family order, they can become stationary, drifting, stormy, and sometimes, destructive to themselves and others. Personality disorders exacerbate the situation and usually professional help is needed, however, if someone doesn't allow the help of parents, sometimes all that can be done is to prepare for the storm and protect oneself from the hurts.

Event Focused Estrangement

In some families, parents have serious events that require intervention by authorities or that lead to estrangement, sometimes temporary, by either adult children or the parent. These situations can be events such as: addictions; criminal arrests; prison; abuse; abandonment; financial exploitation or threats. Although adult children who estrange may have these types of situations; we are hearing more stories of parents being fearful of their adult children and needing protective orders for themselves. These types of estrangements may be necessary for security reasons but even these family situations can usually be met with counseling and support, at least to promote mercy and grace.

Unrealistic Expectations

The final category for discussion in this section is the examination of the conscious mind, particularly for parents. Reading through the thoughts and ideas presented on estrangement, as well as the stages of psychosocial development, do you see any patterns or pictures of yourself? Did you parent with a "pie in the sky" expectation of how everything would turn out? Did you believe the stories in the media or movies on how families should be or could be? Did you ignore your own needs and/or warning signs from children? Do you have a life outside of your children? Did you have your own needs met as a child? Did your own parents try as hard as you wanted them to? Do you feel you are a martyred parent? A needy mom or dad? Can you get out of the role or are you stuck? Does it meet some need to stay stuck? All difficult questions.

Sometimes, it seems parents stay stuck in the situation and ruminate on the loss over and over as a way to keep their child close. It makes some sense if you think about it, but in the long run, it is like a gunshot wound that is just about healed and the patient pulls the bandage off too soon and rolls in the dirt. Perhaps a Greek mythology, Sisyphus-type situation exists of repetitively plodding up a hill, carrying a rock, (the adult estranged child), then rolling it down the hill on purpose, and on top of you. You'll do anything to not leave the rock behind.

And then, I also ask myself and you, do we have it all wrong as parents? Don't all families have some dysfunction? I mean, if you think about it, it's even Biblical, all the way back to Cain and Abel. Speaking of the Bible, Jesus left home and asked twelve disciples to go with him, and they did. However, Jesus was always kind to his mother, Mary. And Moses disappeared for years, only to have a great come back with a certain tablet of commandments.

Maybe, as our children grow up and away, maybe we shouldn't be so connected? Are we supposed to find a new lease on our own lives to enjoy? Perhaps we must learn to let go, let God and let the children find their own way away and then come back to us, if it's meant to be. Perhaps we should be like the pioneers of old, when children took off to settle the West and never saw their parents again. Perhaps children need this to find their own wings. After all, there's a reason the umbilical cord is cut at birth!

Maybe it will all turn out okay!? The point is, most estranged parents try everything to have a healthy relationship with grown children and, in the end, the estranged that have some peace have finally realized they **have** tried everything. And, just perhaps, tried much too hard.

CHAPTER SIX
PERSONAL REFLECTIONS

Briefly Outline what type of story you are currently living. If you have a trusted friend/family member, ask for feedback.

CHAPTER SEVEN
Stepping Out There

Throughout the years of struggle with estrangement issues, feelings of shame, guilt, certainly confusion and anger abound for the parents. As stated, we tend to hide our feelings, make excuses for our grown children, about why we don't see them, why we aren't involved in their lives, why we don't know about health issues or see grandchildren. Parents must OWN their feelings on this issue. For instance, no matter what the estranged child says or how he/she labels the parent, the one fact that cannot be changed is that he/she does have parents...somewhere. There is absolutely no one stronger emotionally than any parent. Claim your place. It's okay to talk about being a parent, even if you never see your adult child. When you get this fact embedded in your heart, you'll feel better.

If our focus stays continuously on the adult child who never calls, the mountain of grief and pain grows and becomes more and more of a reality. Even if there is absolutely no contact, the estranged child lives rent free in our minds, causing hurt and regret, even obsession. I've often thought this may be a natural bond or instinct, since there was never any clear closure such as occurs with a death or a clear understanding on why the child is estranging. I've watched animals defend their young and even search for them if they disappear. Perhaps, it's the same instinctive sign of searching behavior performed by the human parent, as if the child has gone missing or been abducted. This would explain why some parents will drive by houses or schools or search social media to see glimpses of 'missing' children or grandchildren. The tragedy is that the adult child and others ridicule this behavior, or worse, obtain legal papers to block all contact.

Parents, perhaps, have been so overinvolved with their children's lives that even normal separation may appear like estrangement. Its' not that it is the parent's fault, it's just that no life was developed outside of the child. The stories of estrangement from formerly, deeply connected parents are almost like stories from an amputee. The cut off extremity (child) leaves constant phantom limb pain and the parent stays debilitated. The parent remains emotionally dependent on the child who clearly is rejecting them; thus, it is critical for these parents to take some steps toward becoming healthy without the child (for now). It doesn't mean there is no hope. It just means, like on an airplane that depressurizes, the parent must take the whiffs of oxygen first to help the child. It is helpful is to begin to "step out" on the issues slowly, without malice, without retribution, but with honesty and hope. After all, who's heart are we protecting? Instead of worrying how others will receive any information shared about an estranged child, protect your own heart and give glimpses of truth. Most people who know you well already have some idea about the estrangement. Develop statements that explain your life and how you feel. Share some of your story, when questioned, without being hurtful, but without shaming or hurting yourself.

For instance:

"Yes, we have a son. He's married and seems happy, but sadly, we don't see him often."

If questioned more, reveal what you want.

"We would love to see him more. We had a close relationship, but he's chosen less contact."

This may be where you learn who you can trust. If people pursue information with blaming-type questions, be careful (as I say, protect your heart).

If you're asked: "What happened? What did <u>you</u> do?" Then, it's clear what the questioners' perceptions are. You can comment:

"A lot of people don't understand estrangement. While no parent is perfect, many must walk on eggshells with adult children just to keep a relationship."

We have found that this statement often opens up dialogue and revelations from many parents in the same situation. While they may not be totally estranged, many parents are just one opinion, one correction or one refusal from a full-blown estrangement. I often explain to people also how epidemic the problem is currently, along with some of the issues around media and the enabling that perpetuates the problem.

Some estranged parents have chosen to confront the adult child with kind, but clear behavioral expectations, such as: "We will talk or meet with you, however, we must first discuss all the past incidents and hurts."

While, this seems to be a way to step out in truth, it can also be a barrier that no one can step or climb over. In fact, if there is a lot of shame and guilt attached to past incidents, the mind may permanently block any reconciliation. Not to say this is healthy, however, it is a common occurrence. Remember, we started with the information that everyone has filtered memories, thus parental remembered incidents may be the complete opposite of child remembered incidents. In this situation, if you both need to sift through the feelings of who did what and if it is possible to have joint discussion sessions with a spiritual counselor or therapist, it may be helpful. The bottom line is, no matter how someone gets to any potential healing, there will be a point of decision, on both sides, and a need for more understanding about forgiveness, mercy and grace.

FORGIVENESS, MERCY, AND GRACE

Definition:

- FORGIVE: to give up resentment or to claim requital for insult; to cease to feel resentment against an offender.

- To wipe the slate clean.

> *"But if ye forgive not men their trespasses, neither will your Father forgive your trespasses."*
> Matthew 6:15 **(KJV)**

- MERCY: compassionate treatment, clemency, kindness and forgiveness

- GRACE: to honor or favor, unmerited divine assistance given humans for their regeneration or sanctification

"For by grace are ye saved through faith;
and that not of yourselves:
it is the gift of God:[9]
Not of works, lest any man should boast."
Ephesians 2:8-9 (KJV)

TIPS:

- FORGIVENESS does not mean that you are required forget whatever happened to you—after all, that's the point: It happened *to* you. You may not have been vigilant, or may have chosen badly in situations, or have been blinded about a person, situation, bad habit, or addiction. But some act or acts have happened to you that you are now charged to forgive.

- FORGIVENESS does not mean that you condone the hurtful behavior of someone, but that you choose to have empathy and to release the judgment and penalty or revenge toward that person.

- FORGIVENESS can help the offender truly repent, change and can even lead to reconciliation. You can't change the person or undo what happened, but forgiveness can help put the past in perspective and in a context that leads to healing. The emotional pain will then decrease.

> *"Remember ye not the former things,*
> *neither consider the things of old.[19]*
> *Behold, I will do a new thing;*
> *now it shall spring forth; shall ye not know it?*
> *I will even make a way in the wilderness,*
> *and rivers in the desert."*
> Isaiah 43:18–19 (KJV)

- SOMETIMES, we can get stuck in the anger and bargaining phase of loss when we're working on forgiveness. It is important to come to grips with the fact that the past cannot be undone. It is such a simple statement but so hard to disconnect in your heart and mind. However, it helps greatly if the person who hurt you can say, "I wish I could undo what I did to hurt you"—AND REALLY MEAN IT! Of course, God knows our hearts.

- REALIZE that God has let go of your mistakes. He has also let go of the mistakes of others against you. His Son, Jesus, walked the earth in forgiveness. Think of the betrayers and sinners He met, i.e. Judas, Peter, Paul, and Mary Magdalene, to name a few.

> *"Never does the human soul appear so strong*
> *as when it foregoes revenge*
> *and dares to forgive an injury"*
> Edwin Hubbel Chapin

- STAY mindful that some people may use and manipulate a forgiving spirit for their own gains, even your child. Also, check yourself for codependent behaviors. Are you so needy that you find yourself always bonding to people who have problems and take advantage of you? Listen to their words and for surrounding explanations, not excuses for behavior, then read and reread Proverbs. Ask the Holy Spirit to help you stay in wisdom and discernment! Read *"Foolproofing Your Life: An honorable way to deal with the impossible people in your life"*, 1998, by Jan Silvious. It's based on Proverbs.

- MERCY goes hand-in-hand with empathy. It means we see and feel what someone says and does in a manner that allows "walking in their shoes." Are you able to feel another person's pain or struggle? Your mercy alone may open their eyes. Perhaps your adult child needs mercy.

> *"The essence of justice is mercy."*
> Edwin Hubbel Chapin

- MERCY may mean letting the offense and the person go.

- RECIPROCATE: give out the mercy you have received to others.

"Not by works of righteousness which we have done,
but according to his mercy he saved us,
by the washing of regeneration,
and renewing of the Holy Ghost."
Titus 3:5 (KJV)

Grace flows with mercy! God gives it to us for our regeneration. Grace is FREE and must also be given freely by us to others. There is no quid pro quo with grace. There is no blackmail over the offender. When we receive God's grace, none of us totally deserves it—that is why it is called "unmerited favor." Why is grace so totally amazing? It will give you energy, a feeling of cleansing and unconditional love.

> *"And he said unto me, My grace is sufficient for thee:*
> *for my strength is made perfect in weakness.*
> *Most gladly therefore will I rather glory in my*
> *infirmities,*
> *that the power of Christ may rest upon me."*
> 2 Corinthians 12:9 (KJV)

CHAPTER SEVEN
PERSONAL REFLECTIONS

Think about mistakes you have made and the times you needed forgiveness. Can you give yourself mercy? Are you holding grudges against your estranged child or the enablers? Are you able to face them and let them go? Can you start with just one grudge? A Pastor friend of mine once said he was so hurt and upset with someone that he had to ask God to pray for the person because he couldn't even pray. Start there, if needed.

CHAPTER EIGHT
And So, We Wait...

What is the healthiest way to wait for someone we want

in our life? Well, it's as varied as the people who are waiting.

Estrangement is a different, deeper type of grief, and there is

no formula for managing the issue. One reason is because

the person being grieved is still alive and possibly even

causing more problems, pain or refusing to engage to clarify

the issues. Whatever the situation, there is also a fear of

reaching out by all parties, especially if reaching out was previously rejected or ridiculed. However, we need to realize the person IS still alive physically. Depending on the person, the estranged child's heart can still turn, thus hope for parents is still alive.

Some people overthink and intellectualize the issue. Some try to work it to death. Some people become stuck in anger or revenge. Other people live in a dream world, by self-medicating or acting out. There are those who become martyrs/perpetual victims. Many people attribute every problem in their own lives to the estrangement. Some parents give up all together or move on with their lives in a healthy way. That is not to say that most parents don't pass through any or all of these types of behaviors in the process.

Nothing in life is totally under our control. Even though most estranged children have major control issues and think they are in control, none of us are. We can certainly take steps to become healthier and protect our hearts, but anything can still happen! So, as parents, it's important to take an honest assessment of our lives, acknowledge missteps (which most estranged parents have done ad nauseam), define areas of support and comfort and then step forward, one step at a time to feel better. Try this as a start. It's more self-revealing for each Spouse to do separately and then share with each other, if comfortable.

CHAPTER EIGHT
PERSONAL REFLECTIONS
And Estrangement Honest-steps

Step One: Make a timeline of parenting stages. List birth dates, names of children, then list remembered points of the estranged child's life. Record any little event you can remember. If you have been stuck in negative thoughts, using photos may jog positive memories you may have buried.

Step Two: Without beating yourself up, list a few areas where you wish you had known more at the time or wish you had handled something differently.

Step Three: Who is your support? List some of the feelings you currently have about estrangement. Share with spouse/support person. Do you have anyone? If not, can you build a new support group? Even an online one helps! It is critical to have someone to bond with and to share your pain and thoughts. I have found the church or community volunteer groups to be a great place to start. List ONE place to start.

<u>Step Four</u>: List interests you have, besides your estranged child. Even if they are just thoughts, i.e. gardening, art, yoga, golf, singing, writing…anything! Just step out and get involved in something else. Try to express your own truth about estrangement when you begin to trust various people you meet. Record your interests and mark your progress.

For us, we stay busy as we wait. We wait in faith and hope, not in regret and pain. We don't allow others to disrespect our parenting or the time spent working to rebuild relationships. We are involved in helping others understand and deal with marriage and family issues. We have a wonderful, close daughter and son-in-law, grandchildren, grandson-in-law, extended family and two great-grandchildren. We don't pretend with them. We gently discuss the desire to have our son around more in our life. They have questions because they wish their Uncle and his wife were around more too, but there is no angst or negative talk. And sometimes he 'pops' up with them, a text or social media post to them.

Recently, after some sicknesses, tragic family losses, funerals, and weddings, we have reconnected *somewhat* with our estranged son. The caveat is that it is mostly with a few texts and family events. We can talk on birthdays, send cards, and, yes, sometimes it feels awkward with a "walking on eggshells" staccato type communication. Frequently, we have the one-text-one-response behavior from him. The conversations are often on the surface. But we are grateful to know he is alive and healthy; as we are well aware some parents don't have any information. We don't know how he and his wife feel about any of this because we don't talk deeply. In fact, we only scratch the surface of any topic, it's like talking about the weather!

The tragedy of all estrangement behavior for all families is the amount of time lost – the experiences, feelings, situations, joys, hurts, accomplishments and FUN that was missed. Additionally, for most parents, we know that other family members and friends are allowed into the estranged child's world, while the parents are left out. It is a feeling of abandonment and grief that no one can understand unless they have gone through it. It seems so unnatural. It is part of an enigma of life and probably can never be fully understood. It's often not even understood by the estranged child either. So, the question becomes "Why do we try so much to understand it?" Perhaps it is because, as parents, we are programmed to fix things for our family and children. We are programmed to put things back together like we did their broken bicycles, wagons and swings; like the basketball goals and doll houses; like the buttons on jackets and tires on their first cars; like the skinned knees and stitches and report cards and friendships. We were there.

So, in the presence of any pain of separation, we must all remember, we were there for them, even if we messed up at times. We can be grateful for those memories and for the hope of a full reunion that is without regret, judgement or rumination. For now, we can appreciate the brief connections. We are grateful because we aren't groveling for crumbs and we assume that our son and his wife are happy. That's all we can ask for at this time.

It is, after all, what we wanted from the moment of his birth.

CHAPTER NINE
Release Your Heart

Have you ever examined why you may have trouble letting go of something or someone? Why do I feel the need to keep all the notes, cards, papers and mementos of my parenting days? In some ways it's normal for all parents but, in other ways, it feels as if we are trying to prove something. Is it that I was a good Mom? Or to prove I was loved? Or do the papers prove I was hurt? Is it to have a record of my life?

And the biggest question is: Who in the world am I trying to prove it all to and actually…who cares?

"Remember ye not the former things, neither consider the things of old."
Isaiah 43:18 (KJV)

I have boxes that contain notes and cards from my parents and my husband's parents. So many nice thoughts, so many honored memories. I have old family pictures and hundreds of photos of my children and their cousins and events we all participated in. In this digital age, they will probably wind their way into a trash pile, garage sale or even resale shop when we are gone. I rarely look at the pictures, but I'm often the one my grandchildren call to find out who did what and when for school papers or timelines. I guess, in some small, way we all want to leave some memory or footprint for our lives, but sometimes it's best to get them in order and even release some of them. Recently, while looking at old photos of my father (and finding one in front of our old family home) I remembered how he believed in 'living in the now'. I was feeling burdened with trying to figure out what the heck to do with all the pictures and cards I carried around in boxes. In the picture, I swear my dad had a gleam in his eyes!

I heard God speak to me deep in my spirit. *BE GRATEFUL. Open your hands and be GIVING. Release.* Letting go is about forgiveness and mercy. I don't have to keep proof that I was loved by my son—or that I was right or wrong. I don't have to keep proof of what someone said or did. God knows it all anyway, and you know what? Each of us knows our own truths. I don't need to prepare for life in courtroom mode. I don't need to get people back with my words or hang on to hurtful stuff. I need to move forward and release…let it go. Jesus is my Counselor, my Lawyer, anyway. He is always with me. I simply need to forgive everyone involved in the estrangement pattern and show mercy whenever possible, even with the old stuff in my boxes and closets. I pray for a greater ability to let go of hurts and ways to retaliate or my thoughts on how to get even. I pray to be able to sweep my mind of the memories, hurtful words and painful heart lessons.

Again, forgiveness does not mean forgetting or condoning a person's bad choice or behavior. It means releasing self-righteousness and vengeance, and thus valuing an individual as a person. It is not easy because "triggers" or reminders may pop up and allow bad memories or feelings to surface. Sometimes, friends or family will specifically ask you about certain situations causing the event to resurface. Sometimes television programs or movies will remind you of a painful situation and will model an unforgiving or vengeance-filled type of response, causing you to doubt your own forgiveness process. A great reminder: *"Love is an act of constant forgiveness."* As estranged parents, let's model love, whether the child returns it or not.

"For if ye forgive men their trespasses,
your heavenly Father will also forgive you:" Matthew
6:14 (KJV)

So, I looked again at the picture of my earthly father standing by our old family home. It was time. *Let in the light!* I started releasing, tossing, and shredding, opening my clasped, gripped hands, letting go and forgiving! My son is my son. We love him as his parents. He will make his own way. He *has* made his own way successfully. And do you know why? Because we raised him well.

Definition of RELEASE:

- To set free from confinement or bondage (verb)

- Relief from suffering (noun)

"This then is the message which we have heard of him,
and declare unto you,
that God is light,
and in him is no darkness at all."
1 John 1:5 (KJV)

CHAPTER NINE
PERSONAL REFLECTIONS

How do we release, let go, and forgive hurts or evidence of hurts?

How do we do what *is* right instead of trying to *be* right?

I have found out, (the ever-so-hard way), that to let go is to give up pride, give away my perceived right to punish and decide to release the grip any person has on my own heart. Release begins in your own Spirit.

A FIVE-STEP *HAPPY JESUS NURSE* PROCESS OF RELEASE:

1) Begin by asking for God's help and then decide to cooperate with the process.

2) Start with ONE hurtful instance or person and move through the layers. Remember: You aren't responsible for fixing the child or any other person who hurt you, only for forgiving them.

3) Say the following *OUT LOUD* to yourself or a trusted individual and then write it down (you may have to repeat this step for many instances).

"I release (name)

_____

for _____

(be specific about the incident)
And I give (name) to You, God.
Please heal my heart of any pain, anger,
or desire for revenge."

4) Start immediately to let go and let God. Every time any hurtful thoughts come into your mind, replace them, and say, "Okay, I'm letting go GOD".

5) REMIND YOURSELF: We all need forgiveness. Thank God for forgiving you! Give yourself peace.

> "If it be possible, as much as lieth in you,
> live peaceably with all men."
> Romans 12:18 (KJV)

CHAPTER 10
PRESCRIPTION FROM THE RECOVERY ROOM

Is there a prescription for estranged parents? Unfortunately, there is no specific magic pill. Parents will always be moving through the process at differing stages. We have now learned it is a grief process, but the good news is that there are definite recovery steps. We call it developing a *benign detachment.*

1. Surrender your feelings to God. He knows you love your child and that you did your best. He loves you and you are His child. Pray. And pray often. Go to your church, synagogue, community center, Bible Classes, recovery groups or spiritual Yoga…anywhere that connects you to your Higher Power. Don't be afraid of angry feelings. They are normal. Just don't get stuck in them.

2. Surround yourself with others who care for you. Make new friends, even if you have to find strangers every day to give you a smile. I spent a lot of time with my Mom and her caretaker, Joyce, during painful periods of estrangement. Even as she aged and her memory faded, she always understood my feelings. It was amazing, as she would actually ask me about my son, her first grandson. She wasn't afraid to talk about the issue. She was funny, as she would respond: "Darn! Is that still going on?" Additionally, be sure to make healthy plans for yourself during holidays, birthdays and other special times to avoid falling into a "memory-mourning pit."

3. Seek and share ways to help others as much as possible. You can encourage someone else and renew your self-worth. Volunteering has always been in our lives and being a nurse, I usually pulled my family into community activities, such as feeding the homeless or working at a shelter. My husband always makes friends with men on the streets, at neighborhood projects or crisis centers.

There is so much need in the world. Jump in and help. I promise you will feel better!

John distributes food at Community Family Center.

Anne and Grandson Matt feed hungry workers at Thanksgiving.

Mom, (Gerrie), and Joyce visit neighbors.

4. Stay grounded in health and fun. This is tough if you have been rocked by a family break-up or are stuck in "pity/poor me" feelings. We often feel guilty about feeling better! It's what happens when moving through grief. Go to the zoo, the beach, museum, gym or simply go for a stroll. Get exercise. This helps to move through

anger. Even when my Mother couldn't walk, she and her friend Joyce would go visit neighbors!

5. Stop thinking, living in the past, blaming and beating yourself up. Trust me. Your estranged adult child has done enough of that for you. It's so easy to write this, but it is hard to do. Build new, forward thinking memories now!

6. Self-deprecate. It may take a while but try to laugh at yourself through your tears. Sometimes it is pretty funny now for us, as we see ourselves getting jerked around by estrangement control games, like the one-text-one-response game from our son or the passive aggressive I'm-pretending-I-didn't-get-your-phone-call game by his spouse. I pretend, sometimes, that I don't see my spouse and say: "I'm ghosting you," just to break some tension if we are feeling down.

7. Stay away from enablers when you can. Sadly, even if it's family, especially the passive-aggressive kind who say they don't want to take sides. Parents don't want sides. When someone says that to you, they are probably betrayers and have already taken a side and it's not yours! Remember: Some people enjoy your pain, as it makes them feel better about their own. That's just another sad fact of life.

8. Scrutinize your own heart as much as possible. Don't make decisions out of spite or revenge. I'm not saying I haven't done this, just advising that it doesn't usually work out. It builds more regrets. Try to remain quiet, if in a family situation. If you're afraid you'll be tempted to go off on someone, go into another room, go outside or just leave if it's too painful.

9. Schedule downtime for yourself. Rest, read, pray and exercise You ARE worth it! Sometimes, the best gift I give myself is a nap.

10. SCREAM, if needed, but then SING. You're a survivor. As my well-known preacher says all the time, "Be a victor, not a victim".

POSTSCRIPT

As we separated ourselves from the painful behavior of constantly seeking a relationship with our son, some successful contact was made. Presently, our journey with the issues of adult child estrangement is on a more stable, though not consistent, ride. We visited with him several months ago but sometimes we go months with no contact. We can text or contact our son and daughter-in-law periodically and they sometimes reciprocate in kind. We still *walk on eggshells* at times but then he may also. We exchange birthday and other greeting cards and we can handle some family events without feeling left out or dismissed (even if we are). We *try* not to take anything personally. By this I mean we don't perseverate over things or desire to rehash any hurts. We substitute the desire for what we had in the past, that is, a deeper relationship built on sharing current information and feelings, with other friendships and family in our lives. Our son may not realize what he has lost, but we do. We pray that, perhaps someday, he will seek a closer relationship with us.

Suggested Resources and Readings

This is a gentle invitation for any in need of information or support from other experienced estranged parents. The following online support group is most helpful. It is only accessed via Facebook and Posts can be anonymous.

Support Page for Parents of Adult Estranged Children

Books for Education, Healing and Health:

Benson, Herbert, M.D., (1996) *Timeless Healing, the POWER and BIOLOGY of BELIEF*, Scribner, New York. (Relaxation and Healing)

Catholic Book of Prayers, (2001) edited by Rev. Maurus Fitzgerald, O.F.M., Catholic Book Publishing Co., New Jersey.

Any Bible!! King James to NIV

Erikson, Erik H., *Childhood and Society* (Theory of Psychosocial Development), 1950, W.W. Norton, New York (1*)

Helton RN, BSN, MS, Anne Stewart, *Happy Jesus Nurse: Heart*
Lessons (Amazon.com)

Keller, Tim, (2008) *The Reason for God*, Dutton, New York.

Leaf, Caroline, (2013) *SwitchOnYourBrain*, Baker Books, Michigan.

Lucado, Max, (2012) *Grace*, Thomas Nelson, Nashville, Tennessee. Maxlucado.com

McGregor, Sheri (2016) *Done with the Crying: Help and Healing for Mothers of Estranged Children*. Sowing Creek Press, San Marcos, California.

Moore, Beth, (2009) *Get Out of that Pit,* Thomas Nelson Publisher, TN.

Neeld, Elizabeth Harper, Ph.D., (2003) *Seven Choices: Finding Daylight after Loss Shatters Your World,* Warner Books, New York.

Silvious, Jan, (1998) *Fool-Proofing Your Life, An Honorable Way to Deal with the Impossible People in Your Life*, Waterbrook Press.

Terkeurst, Lysa, (2012) *Unglued,* Zondervan, Michigan.

APPENDIX

Comments and thoughts from the experts (the estranged parents) on

"Erased Memories" Chapter.

Trish says: *Well worth the read, everything resonated with me. Thank you so much for giving me the words to articulate my journey.*

Nina says: *Same story, Only it's my daughter 8 years of walking dead.*

Tiff says: *Thank you, this is all so real and so true. Help me Jesus.*

Su says: *Wow!! Thank you so much for this! Our son estranged from us 16 months ago and this describes it perfectly. I've grieved and am moving on, but it is definitely like a slow bleed.*

Em says: *Impressive writing. I've never read something on this disorder so well written. Unfortunately, I have one of those sons who chooses to believe in his make-believe world. I decided not to be a part of it ever again. It's been over 10 yrs. now since I've seen or talked to him. Thank you for putting into words what I have only had scrambled puzzle pieces floating in my head trying to put together and make sense of. What you wrote makes total sense.*

K says: *Thank you for this. Our youngest daughter snuffed us out of her life 2-1/2 years ago. It has destroyed our small family...she took our only granddaughter... We try to enjoy life – we have friends, relatives etc. who do care. Having said that, we wake up each day hurting and missing our daughter. We are in our late 70's – we know Jesus as our Savior. We know He is walking with us in this... just want peace.*

<u>To all commenters</u>: *Let's all stay in Peace and remember: Take good care of yourselves. I am keeping you all covered in peaceful prayers....***Anne**

AUTHOR BIO

Anne Stewart Helton is a wife, mom, and grandmother. She's a Registered Nurse for over 40 years, has a Bachelor of Science in Nursing and Masters-of-Science in Community Health Nursing. She has taught Community Health at University of Texas Nursing School and has primarily worked with vulnerable populations. She did the early research on Battering During Pregnancy and worked with the March of Dimes to develop and implement programs for pregnant women and teens. She has written and produced PBS-TV productions on HIV/AIDS, Child Abuse, and Grief and is author of *Happy Jesus Nurse: Heart Lessons*, on family and marriage. Currently, Anne enjoys reading, writing, Bible classes, gardening, volunteering and long walks with her husband John and their dog Sheila! She especially cherishes time with her family.

Made in the
USA
Columbia, SC